Alveston

By John Richard Hodges

John Richard Hodges

For Nick - *A Remarkable Young Man-1979-1998*

There are many people

who come and go in our lives,

a few touch us in ways

that change us forever.

You have made a difference

in my life and I am grateful.

John Richard Hodges ~ 2017

Contents:

Front piece:

Dedication:

Contents Sheet:

Foreword:

FOREWORD

For most of the first 20 years of my life Alveston Manor was my home. My father bought the manor house from the Reverend Fortescue, and MP Eric Barnard, a prominent Stratford figure and much respected Auctioneer handled the sale.

It was a marvellous and exciting building for young boys to have as their own playground. My younger brother Brian and I knew every inch of the property. We explored the lofts above the ceilings, found hundreds of sparrows' nests, climbed all over the roofs, walked along the ridges, slid through hidden trapdoors into cellars having to cut through thick curtains of ancient cobwebs, excavated behind the filbert-nut avenue for the remains of a Roman villa, crawled into the underground well chamber which controlled the water supply from the river to the monastic stew ponds and climbed the two magnificent cedars, In all, the fifteen acres of the Manor's property was a wonderland playground for Brian and me.

I mention just Brian and myself because my elder brother Tommy spent six years in the Navy and just a few years living at the Manor before he married. My eldest sister Pauline served in the Wrens then married fairly quickly whilst Margaret was with us very briefly before marrying and going to America.

During the war years the property was requisitioned for the use of the Canadian Armed Forces, mainly Airmen. When the War ended and the Manor was handed back to us it was in a state of dereliction. The house was in need of a major restoration and the grounds overgrown and there was a mountain of waste by the tennis courts. I must not lead you to believe that it was all play and no work for my brother Brian and me.

My parents took on the major task to restore the property and at the same time convert it into a hotel which my mother had decided to run. So Brian and I were found many jobs to do such as helping the builders with their restoration work by cleaning the Elizabethan bricks recovered from the Manor's walled vegetable gardens and even some from bombed ancient buildings in Coventry. When we became older we were trained as waiters, kitchen workers and hall porters. On school holidays in the tourist season we were kept very busy. It took over a year to restore the property which my mother then ran as a hotel which she did with much success.

Without John Hodges the author of this work, the Alveston Manor story would probably have never been recorded therefore Stratford-upon-Avon and particularly the Bird family have much to thank him for.

John, son of a Shropshire farmer, was educated at Bedstone College Ludlow and, after an early career with a leading publishing house in St James, London, ultimately decided that his vocation was for teaching. He took a degree and teaching certificates at Christ's College in Liverpool and thereafter his teaching career took him across the world, particularly in the Middle East in Jeddah, Saudi Arabia and Paphos in Cyprus, and he has travelled extensively. He is currently a part-time tutor and teacher.

John Hodges in his carefully researched history of Alveston Manor meticulously delves into the fascinating past of this beautiful Tudor house. John's work on this house and of several others in the area upon which John has researched, is so important because without doubt the histories and the more intimate facts concerning these special properties would be lost forever.

John's passion for his work as an author interested in historic properties lacking a properly recorded history will manifest itself when you read this book and hopefully some of the others, for example, the histories of the Welcombe and Ettington Park Hotels. You will find the books fascinating and interesting particularly if you live in this part of South Warwickshire and of course in Stratford-upon-Avon where these wonderful properties as hotels play a major role in catering for the higher end of the tourist market.

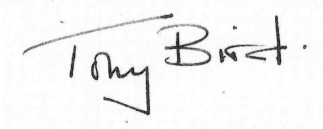

Tony Bird OBE - 2017

Chapter One: Early History

An early engraving of the Cathedral Church of Worcester c1724: - courtesy of the Dean and Chapter of Worcester Cathedral©

Alveston was held by the church of Worcester from at least the 10th until the 16th century. We know that Bishop Oswald in 966 made a grant of 3 hides here to Eadric his thegn and another of 5 hides to the same Eadric in 985. In the following century, however, the church nearly lost possession. The 15 hides(Hide: Measurement of land for tax assessment. Approximately 120 acres, depending on local variations in the acre), at which the manor was rated in the Domesday Book, were in the reign of the Confessor held in equal portions by *Bricstuin* and by *Britnod* and *Alwi*. By 1086 Bricstuin's moiety(each of two parts into which a thing is or can be divided) had descended to his six sons, who, while admitting that Archbishop Aldred (who had been the Bishop of Worcester from1046-62), had enjoyed certain rights over the land, were unable to say whether their father had held it of the church or of Earl Leofric. For themselves, they claimed to be able *'to betake themselves with the land whither they would'* and to hold of the earl. As to Britnod and Alwi, the Domesday Commissioners reported that *'the county knows not of whom they held.'* Bishop Wulfstan, however, maintained his title before Queen Matilda, secured a confirmation from the king, and in 1089 granted the 15 hides to his monastery at Worcester.

One of the fine stained glass windows from Alveston Manor Hotel showing Bishop Wulfstan maintaining his title to the Manor before Queen Matilda in 1089: - JRH©

The monks obtained from Henry I a reduction from 15 to 10 hides in the assessment for geld and from Henry III, in 1255, a grant of free warren(a piece of land set aside for breeding game, especially rabbits) in their demesne(a piece of land attached to a manor retained by the owner for their own use). Although the manor was in the bishop's liberty of Pathlow, the right of sheriffs tourn here was stated in 1240 to belong to the Earls of Warwick.

In Sir William Dugdale's 17ᵗʰ century book '*The Antiquities of Warwick*' Volume 2, page 674 the following Alveston reference to the time of Richard II appears:

Richard II of England – 1367 - 1400

'And in the 15th year of the reign of Ric.2nd on the feast of St. Michael the Archangel, John Green then Prior, and his Chapter, granted to John at Halle de Alveston, and Alice his wife, their Manor of Alveston for the term of 20 years, at the yearly rent of ten quarter of wheat, thirty quarter of barley, payable between the Feasts of St. Michael the Archangel, and the Annunciation of Our Lady, and six shillings and four pence for the 'Fifhery'; besides four bushels of wheat to the 'Elemosinary', and to the 'Coquinary' 8 hogs, price 24s., 20 geese, price 6s. 8d. 20 hens, price 3s. 4d. and 200 eggs, price 10d.' –

The *Elemosinary* is who we call today the monk in charge of alms to the poor at the Cathedral priory, otherwise known as the *Almoner*. Similarly the *Coquinary is* Dugdale's transcription of *Coquinarius* – the monk in charge of the catering, otherwise known as the *Kitchener.* In the 15th year of his reign was June 1391-June 1392.

Other references to Alveston found in the Worcester Cathedral library have included the following:

1. From the *Worcester Liber Albus* WCM A5 (1301-1450) folio 104a dated 1321: A document in French which appears to be an agreement between the Prior and monks of Worcester Cathedral with John de Carletone for a mill at Tydyngton in the monks' manor of Alveston in the reign of Edward II – he must repair/build at his own cost (including the sluices).

A 14th century mill and watermill: - courtesy of the British Library©

2. From the *Worcester Monastic register* WCM A6 (i) (1458-1498) folio 73 – The 'farm' at Alveston is indentured to John Askell and his sons Thomas and William in the reign of King Edward IV (was the King of England from 4th March 1461 until 3rd October 1470, and again from 11th April 1471 until his death in 1483. He was the first Yorkist King of England).This means that the monks let it out to Askell and his sons and then just collected the rent from them.

Farming in the 14th Century taken from the Luttrell Psalter: - courtesy of the British Library©

3. From the WCM A6 (i) folio 6v: in 1459 a watermill was let by the monks at the farm of Alveston to William Crowley, John Crowley and William de Wotton of Hanley *(Thanks to Cathedral Library volunteer Vanda Bartoszuk for researching these sources).*

14ᵗʰ Century Watermill showing the eel trap baskets

Dr David Morrison, the librarian at Worcester Cathedral Library, has found early document references to the Priory at Worcester and Alveston Manor at Stratford. These include B15, B24 & B25.

The manor came into the King's hands at the Dissolution, but was granted to the newly established Dean and Chapter of Worcester in 1542. Three years later it was regranted to the Crown, together with other property, by the Dean and Chapter in return for being relieved of the obligation under their statutes to maintain twelve divinity students at Oxford.

B25 in the Cathedral Library refers to Henry's son Edward VI and is dated 27ᵗʰ June 1552:

'Memorandum in which it is ordered that the Dean *and* Chapter be discharged of a debt of £26.12.8. for arrears of rent from the manor of

Alveston, co. Warw., the manor of Icombe, co. Glos., and the parsonage of Doderhill, co. Worcs., unpaid at the Feast of the Annunciation 36 Henry VIII (1545), land which the Dean and Chapter had given to the King in consideration from the exhibition of 12 students at the Universities.'

* *

One of the first buildings on the site of the Alveston Manor Hotel was thought to be an Anchorite cell, circa 960. Later, a small monastery was built by the monks of Worcester. The same monks erected the first wooden bridge to improve the original ford that was used to cross the river.

A small Anglo-Saxon monastery similar to the one which may have been at Alveston

THE BUILDING OF ALVESTON MANOR BY THE MONKS

One of the stained glass windows at the Alveston Hotel depicting the history of the Manor: - JRH©

An anchorite or anchoret (female anchoress) was a religious hermit who wished to retire from the world, so that it was possible to live an intensely prayer-orientated, ascetic and if circumstances permitted, Eucharist focused life.

The anchorites were required to take a vow of stability of place, going instead for permanent enclosures which were often attached to churches or monasteries. Sometimes they were actually bricked up with only a window for access to food or to get rid of waste.

They were subject to a religious rite of consecration that closely resembled the funeral rite, following which – theoretically, they would be considered dead to the world, a type of living saint. Anchorites had certain autonomy, as they did not answer to any ecclesiastical authority other than the bishop and at Alveston this would have been the Bishop of Worcester.

An icon of St Anthony the Great, father of Christian Monasticism

Early Anglo-Saxon burials and cremation remains have been found on the site of *Alveston Manor*. In 2007 the *Warwickshire Museum Field Service* carried out the osteological analysis of two incomplete skeletons, two disarticulated and two cremated bone assemblages from the *Alveston Hotel* (NGR SP 2087 5473). The remains were recovered in 2002 during an archaeological evaluation prior to the construction of a new health club at the hotel. The burials derived from an area immediately to the south-west of an Anglo-Saxon cremation and inhumation cemetery excavated in 1934 and 1971. The burials from the previous phases of excavation contained mostly children and young adults and were poorly preserved. The two inhumation burials (Skeleton 425 and 198) from the 2002 excavations were thought to date to the Anglo-Saxon period. Both burials contained grave goods dating from the period. The date of the cremation burials was less certain, but also thought to date from this same period. Some of the objects recovered from the burials included a Penannular brooch – (a Celtic brooch, more properly called the pennannular brooch and its closely related type, the pseudo-penannular brooch, are types of brooch clothes fasteners, often very large).

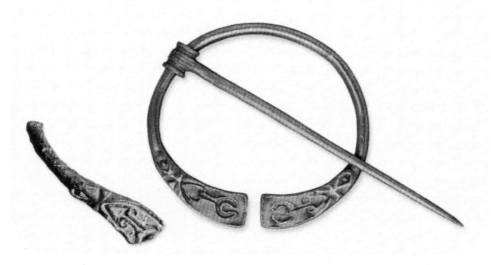

An example of a pennannular brooch- this is a 6ᵗʰ century fragment brooch with enamel on the flared terminals from Dinas Powys, Wales, shown with an artist's reconstruction

Other grave goods recovered included glass beads, a knife, spearheads and a buckle.

The cremated bones were generally well burnt causing the complete loss of the organic portion of the bone and producing a buff to white colour in both of the burials uncovered. According to McKinley (1989), the body requires a minimum temperature of 500 degrees Celsius over seven to eight hours to achieve complete calcination of the bone.

****

The Parish of Alveston lies to the east of Stratford, between the Avon and the Banbury Road, and is bounded on the west by Charlecote, Loxley and Alderminster. It was included in the borough in 1924. Its present boundaries seem to be approximately those given in the Saxon charter of 985. The parish includes two separate villages of Alveston and Tiddington and part of the hamlet of Bridgetown, with the Manor House, which was once the residence of the *Lanes* and the *Bishops.*

Roman remains and occupation have been found at nearby Tiddington as well as the evidence of Saxon occupation both here and at Alveston. At Tiddington a Roman settlement on the golf links south of Oaks Farm was excavated from 1925-7. The remains included a tile kiln, ore roasting and iron smelting furnaces and cupels for smelting lead; and the range of coins from Claudius to Honorius indicate a prolonged occupation, which may have survived the withdrawal of the legions in the 5ᵗʰ century.

Roman Imperial coins from the time of Claudius

* *

Chapter Two: Later History of the Manor

Alveston Manor: - courtesy of the Shakespeare Birthplace Trust©-DR272-1830

The **Manor of Alveston** was held by the Bishops of Worcester from the c10th to the c16th century. In 1562 Elizabeth I granted the **manor of Alveston** to Edward Williams and Ralph Browne of the Inner Temple, agents for Sir Ambrose Cave, to whom they sold it for £1,007 (c£171,492 today) a few weeks later; and he sold it again in the following year to Ludovic Greville of Milcote. On Greville's death in 1589 his estates passed to his son Sir Edward Greville, who is afterwards referred to as having held lands at Alveston of the Crown by military service. He sold the **manor** in 1603 to Richard Lane of Bridgetown, son of that Nicholas Lane whose effigy is in the old church of Alveston.

The Old Church at Alveston

Nicholas Lane's effigy in the Old Church, Alveston

Lane died in 1613. His son Edward (1589-1625) sold the **Alveston Manor** estate to his brother-in-law, Richard Bishop of Cholsey near Wallingford. Bishop was knighted and became a justice of the peace for the county after the Restoration and died at the age of 88 in 1673. His son William (1626-1700) succeeded him. He was knighted in 1678 and having no issue, bequeathed the **manor** to his nephew Hugh Brawn, son of his sister Elizabeth Brawn, rector of Saintbury. Hugh Brawn left a son of the same name, who succeeded him, and three daughters: Elizabeth, who married Charles Knottesford of Studley in 1712; Theodosia, married in 1721 to John Fortescue of Cookhill and of Gray's Inn, London; and Judith, who remained unmarried. Hugh Brawn the younger died on the 24th April 1767 and the **manor** then came to his sister Judith and his nephew John Knottesford. The estate by this time consisted of little more than the **manor house at Bridgetown** and the surrounding fields. In the inclosure of 1772 there were no manorial rights to be compensated and the allotment to Miss Brawn and her nephew for their holding in the open fields of the manor was only 1 rood and 13 perches. Knottesford was sole **lord of the manor** by 1776. On his death he devised it in trust for his kinsman Francis Fortescue, then a minor, who took the additional name of Knottesford as a condition of his succeeding to the estate. The Rev. Francis Knottesford-Fortescue lived at the **manor house** until his death in 1859. His great-grandson, the Rev. J. N. Fortescue, vicar of Wilmcote, sold the estate in c1938. It then comprised the **manor house** and about 150 acres of land.

The three Censuses which mention the Fortescue-Knottesford family are the 1841, 1851 and the 1881. These make for some interesting reading concerning a Victorian family household and their servants:

The 1841 Census – Alveston Manor - Alveston

Francis Knottesford	Age 69	Clergyman	Born in this County: No
Maria "	66	Wife	No
Edward Fortescue	25	Clergyman	No
Francis "	22		No
Maria "	31		No
6 Female Servants		Servants	
Edward "	1		Yes
1 more female and 2 male servants		Servants	

The Rev. Francis Fortescue-Knottesford -1772-1859

1851 Census Alveston – Bridgetown Manor House

Francis Fortescue Knottesford	Head – Married - 78	Rector of Billesley	Born Edmonton
Maria F. Knottesford	Wife - 75		Ovington-Essex
Maria M. Jackson	Daughter - 40		Suffolk – Stoke by Nayland
Mary G. Jackson	Grand Daughter - 5		Alcester -Warks
Georgina F. Jackson	Grand Daughter - 4		" "

Henrietta Jackson	Grand Daughter - 2			" "
Catherine M. Jackson	Grand Daughter – 5 months			Alcester - Warks
George Fortescue	Son - 3			" "
Vincent Fortescue	Son - 2			" "

Plus Housekeeper, 2 housemaids, 1 kitchen maid, 4 nurses, 1 butler & 1 footman

1881 Census Alveston – Manor House

Edward F. H. Fortescue	Head –Captain in the Army-Half Pay	Married	41	Born in Alveston-Warks
Alicia M. "	Wife	Wife	42	Dorset
Francis G. "	Daughter		9	Switzerland- Lausanne
Maria J. "	"		7	" "
John N. "	Son		6	Hampstead- Middlesex
Faithful E. "	Son		3	" "
Alice A. James	Governess		19	Calais - France
4 Other female Servants	1 housemaid, 1 domestic nurse, 2 domestic servants and 1 trained nurse.	Servants		

The Coat of Arms as shown on a bookplate of the Rev. Francis Fortescue Knottesford: - courtesy of the Shakespeare Birthplace Trust Archives©

An article appeared in The Times for the 5th March 1910 relating to Faithful Edward Fortescue:

KNOTTESFORD-FORTESCUE –On the 23d February at Ifon, Southern Nigeria, FAITHFUL EDWARD, B.A., Brasenose College, Oxford, Barrister-at-Law, Lincoln's Inn, Assistant District Commissioner, S. Nigeria, aged 32, youngest son of the late Major E. F. Knottesford-Fortescue, J.P., of **Alveston Manor,** *Stratford-upon-Avon, and Mrs Knottesford-Fortescue, of 45 Banbury Road, Oxford. Served in 40th Company, 10th Battalion I.Y. South African War.*

Aiden Nichols in his book *The Latin Clerk: The Life and Work and Travels of Adrian Fortescue* gives us an insight into the Fortescue family and their connections with **Alveston Manor**:

'Adrian Fortescue belonged to a gentry family with strong clerical connections in the Anglican establishment. His father Edward Bowles Knottesford Fortescue (1816-1877), was born at Stoke-by-Nayland in Surrey, the son of Francis Fortescue and Maria Fortescue, nee Downing (her father George Downing, was rector of Ovington and a prebendary of Ely Cathedral. Francis Fortescue (1772-1859) had taken Orders in the Church of England, as would his son. But thanks to the testamentary arrangements of his godfather, he became a wealthy man. A condition of the inheritance was adding 'Knottesford' the surname of his benefactor to his own. In 1823 the couple moved with (at this point) their two sons George and Edward to the family estate at **Alveston Manor,** *then on the outskirts of Stratford-on-Avon, where Francis lived as a 'squarson' acting as the rector of the parish of Billesley, some five miles from their home.'*

Billesley Church, Warwickshire

There is some evidence that there was an earlier church on the site of the present church which dated back to the 12th century. The present church was built in 1692 by Bernard Whalley. Alterations were made to the church in the 18th century. The church served the now abandoned medieval village of Billesley until its population declined in the 15th century and also served the owners of the nearby Billesley Hall.

The present Billesley Manor Hotel formerly Billesley Hall, alongside the church of All Saints

There is a tradition that William Shakespeare married Anne Hathaway in the earlier church on the site, and that Shakespeare's granddaughter Elizabeth Barnard was married there. However, as the parish registers have not survived, this cannot be confirmed.

Elizabeth Hall, the granddaughter of William Shakespeare with her first husband Thomas Nash.

Thomas Nash: 1593-1647 – was the first husband of Elizabeth Barnard. He had lived most of his life in Stratford, and was the dominant male figure amongst Shakespeare's senior family line after the death of Dr John Hall, Shakespeare's son-in-law in 1635.

Portrait of Thomas Nash

Thomas was called to the bar on 25th November 1623, but there is no evidence he actually practised law. The *Oxford Dictionary of National Biography* states that he may, however have taken over the role his father held in being an agent for Sir John Hubaud, a High

Sheriff of Warwickshire, but Sir John had died in 1583, ten years before Thomas was born.

When Thomas's father died in 1622, he was bequeathed properties close by the **Alveston Manor**. He received *The Bear Inn*, which is close by the *Swan's Nest* across the road from the present Alveston Manor Hotel a house in Bridge Street, and a piece of land called 'the Butt close by the Avon' where burghers used to shoot at archery butts. Thomas was the executor to his father's will. It appears that Thomas held onto the *Bear Inn*, and we know from records that his father-in-law Dr John Hall once treated someone that he called one of Thomas's servants *lying at the Bear*, presumably indicating that he was a publican or worker at that inn. Dr Hall's first treatment for the poor heavily jaundiced servant elicited 'seven vomits', and this and further treatments 'cured him perfectly.'

The Swan's Nest and the Bear opposite the Alveston Hotel: - JRH©

* *

The 1901 Census shows a Samuel Sanders living at the Manor House – he and his family had rented the Manor.

1901 Census Alveston – Manor House

Samuel Sanders	Head	Company Director	55 M	Tavistock - Devon
Isabel J. "	Wife		54M	Down Hatherley - Glos
Isabel M. "	Daughter		28 S	Warwickshire
Arthur B. "	Son	Solicitor	26 S	Malvern Hills - Worcester
Douglas B. "	Son	Metal Merchant	25 S	Warwickshire
Muriel G. "	Daughter		22 S	"
Gladys S. "	Daughter		19 S	Snitterfield - Warwickshire
Isabel J. "	Daughter		7	" "
Lily Snodgrass			39 S	Melbourne - Australia
Grace R. Hawking	Servant	Nurse	48 S	St Ives - Cornwall
Mary A. Howard	Servant	Cook	33 S	Worcester
G. E. Reid	Servant	Housemaid	26 S	Stratford-upon-Avon
Sarah Williams	Servant	Housemaid	20 S	Warwick
Annie Hickman	Servant	Kitchenmaid	15 S	Dunchurch - Warwick
Wallis H	Servant	General	18 S	Wolverton - Warwick
Arthur S. Davis	Servant	Butler	30 S	Kidderminster- Worc.

It is interesting to note that all the servants were single and came from quite different parts of the country and also included one from Australia. Families liked to employ single servants who lived a distance away from the family home so that no gossip could be spread locally!

* *

The history of Alveston Manor is quite complicated as the manor was rented out on various occasions and also in the various census returns there is some confusion for research, for example, the original Lord of the Manor lived on the site of what is now 'Alveston House' two miles distant. By 1811 the Alveston Manor Hotel building was known as 'Bridgetown House' and by 1851 it was 'Bridgetown Manor House.' By 1881 it was simply 'The Manor House.'

Returning to the earlier history of Alveston Manor in more detail we have the interesting character of:

Sir Ambrose Cave: (1502 - 2nd April 1568)

Sir Ambrose Cave owned **Alveston Manor** for a short time. He was an English politician and the son of Richard Cave and Margaret Saxby of Stanford, Northamptonshire. He was educated at Cambridge University and knighted by 1525.

He was a Member of Parliament for Leicestershire in 1545, 1547 and 1553 and for Warwickshire in 1549. He was Chancellor of the Duchy of Lancaster (1558-1569) and 'Custos Rotulorum' of Warwickshire (also 1558-1568).

Custos Rotulorum – *in England and Wales, the principal Justice of the Peace of a county, who has nominal custody of the records of the commission of the peace. The function is usually fulfilled by the Lord Lieutenant.*

He married Margery Willington the daughter of William Willington. Their daughter married Sir Henry Knollys, a privateer and MP. His nephew Roger Cave married Margaret, a sister of *William Cecil, 1ˢᵗ Baron Burghley*, the great minister who rose to great prominence under Elizabeth I.

A Privateer – *was a private person or ship that engaged in maritime warfare under a commission of war. Elizabeth I encouraged such persons as Sir Henry Knolly. The commission also known as a 'letter of marque', employed the person to carry on all forms of hostility permissible at sea by the usages of war, including attacking foreign ships during wartime and taking them as prizes. Captured ships, as with the Spanish ships under Elizabeth, were subject to condemnation and sale under prize law with the proceeds divided between the privateer sponsors, ship owners and the crew.*

William, 1ˢᵗ Baron Burghley great minister of Elizabeth I, by unknown artist: - NPG – 362©

Burghley House in Lincolnshire the grand country house of Lord Burghley

Sir Ambrose Cave was born at Stanford on Avon and died at the same place in 1568. He is buried in a fine table tomb in the Church of St Nicholas at Stanford-on-Avon.

HERE·LYETH·THE·BODIE·OF·SIR·AMBROSE·CAVE·KNIGHT
SOM·TYME·CHAVNCELOR·OF·THE·DVCHY·OF·LANCASTER
AND·ONE·OF·THE·MOST·HONORABLE·PRIVE·COVNSEL
TO·OVR·SOVERAIGNE·LADIE·QVEENE·ELIZABETH·
WHO·DEPARTED·THIS·LIEF·THE·SECOND·OF·APRIL·
ANNO·DOMINI·1568:·

Ludovic Greville –

In 1577 Ludovic was lord of the manor of Welford; he was a member of an important Warwickshire family, cousin of the Grevilles of Beauchamp Court, Alcester (ancestors of the Earls of Warwick). He seems to have agreed on a partial enclosure of the open field land at Welford, in which a number of villagers resigned their rights over '*enclosures of Grevyll lately digged,*' in exchange for purchasing their copyright lands; (information from the Deeds in Warwickshire County Records Office.)

Enclosure *(sometimes inclosure), was the legal process during the 18ᵗʰ century when landowners could enclosure or take over common land or small landownings to create one large farm or estate. Under 'enclosure', such land is fenced (enclosed) and deeded or entitled to one or more owners.*

The deeds in the Warwickshire County Archives Office say nothing of the shocking deeds of Ludovic Greville. According to Dugdale (1728 edition, Vol II, 705f), he coveted the property of a former servant, Richard Webb, and had forged a will in his own favour, and then had Webb murdered. Later '*one of the assassinates, being in his cups at Stratford, dropped out some words amongst his pot companions that it lay within his power to hand his master.*'

He in turn was hastily despatched but the crimes were exposed and Greville was tried for his crime on 6ᵗʰ November 1589. To prevent the loss of his estates, he remained mute throughout the trial and was pressed to death, and '*lands of great worth in both Gloucestershire and Warwickshire passed to his eldest son Edward Greville.*'

This story may not have been completely accurate as the deed entitled CR2028/45/3/1/4 shows that in 1591, the Welford estate was in the hands of Queen Elizabeth. Thus it must have been forfeited to the Crown, although presumably later restored to Ludovic's son Edward.

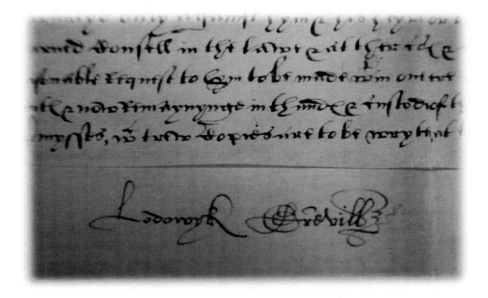

Part of the Will of Ludovic Greville and his elaborate signature: - courtesy of the Warwickshire County Records Office reference CR 2028/45/3/3©

Edward was the cousin of Fulke Greville, and it appears that the family status was sufficient for him to return as a knight of the shire despite his father's infamy and the hatred to which he was himself regarded by 1593.
Being the cousin of Fulke Greville may have had an influence on Edward being returned his inheritance.

Fulke Greville, 1ˢᵗ Baron Brook, 13ᵗʰ Baron Latimer and 5ᵗʰ Baron Willoughby de Broke 1554-1628 – was an Elizabethan poet, dramatist and statesman who sat in the House of Commons at various times between 1581 and 1621, when he was raised to the peerage.

Sir Fulke Greville, 1ˢ Baron Brook

There is an interesting story connected with Warwick Castle that in 1628 Greville was stabbed at the castle by Ralph Haywood, a servant, who believed that he had been cheated in his master's will.

Haywood then turned the knife on himself. Greville's physicians treated his wounds by filling them with pig fat rather than disinfecting them. The pig fat turned rancid and infected the wounds, and he died in agony four weeks after the attack. Sir Fulke Greville is buried in the Collegiate Church of St Mary, Warwick in a splendid tomb. The epitaph on the tomb had been composed by Greville himself:

Folk Greville
Servant to Queene Elizabeth
Conceller to King James
And frend to Sir Philip Sidney.
Trophaeum Peccati

Sir Fulke Greville's Tomb in St Mary's Collegiate Church, Warwick

In his splendid book 'Haunted Castles of Britain and Ireland' Richard Jones tells the story of the ghost of Fulke Greville which is still said to haunt Warwick Castle:

"For those who come to this epitome of English castles seeking encounters of a more spine-tingling nature, the 'Ghost Tower' is the place to visit. Sir Fulke Greville was granted Warwick Castle by King James I in 1604. At the time, the place had been unoccupied for 14 years and was in a ruinous condition. Fortunately, Greville, as well as a being a fine poet and playwright, was a rich and influential man, who slowly converted Warwick Castle into 'the most princely seat within the midlands part of this realm'. Greville served as Chancellor of the Exchequer from 1614 to 1621. He was later raised to the peerage as Baron Brooke, and then appointed Commissioner of the Treasury.

Seven years later, thoughts of his own mortality led Greville to draw up a will. He had never married and had no children, so he decided to make slight provision for his servant, Ralph Haywood. Haywood was not impressed with the paltry bequest and, in a fit of rage, stabbed his master while helping him dress at his house in London. It took the unfortunate Greville a month to die, his agony compounded by the surgeon's insistence on packing the wound with pig fat.

He was brought back to Warwick Castle, and his tomb can still be seen in nearby St. Mary's Church. Greville's ghost returns to the castle to walk the room that was once his study. Here witnesses have reported catching fleeting glimpses of his sad shade staring at them from the dark corners, or feeling his presence at the place where he once composed such prophetic lines as:

If nature did not take delight in blood,
She would have made more easy ways to good."

The Ghost Tower at Warwick Castle

* *

Nothing very much is known about Edward Greville's upbringing and early life, except for an unsubstantiated story that he had killed one of his elder brothers accidentally. After his father's trial and death, Edward inherited his father's estates and these he wasted utterly, and as his only son John died before him, this branch of the family became extinct.

Greville was clearly detested by the corporation of Stratford upon Avon. He revived a claim to control the election of the bailiff, and another to dispose of the office of town crier and collector of market tolls. He asserted that the toll corn belonged to him being the **Lord of the Manor**. The corporation was not happy and several of its members armed with matlocks, shovels and spades, broke into an enclosure called Bankcroft, levelled the hedges and mounds, drove in horses, oxen, kine, swine and hoggerels, and according to Greville, '*did depasture, tread down and consume to the value of 40s.; and willows did lop and the wood thereof carried away... and other enormities to him did do.*'

They were arrested for riot, and the ensuing lawsuit dragged on for some time. On another occasion the Privy Council reproved him for making difficulties over certain services it required, and for not being present in Warwickshire to perform them. Greville is also remembered for the magnitude of his debt which accumulated at least from the early years of the seventeenth century, when he began to sell his property. In about 1609 he parted with the **manor of Stratford**. The greater part of his property, including Milcote, was bought by his son-in-law, Sir Arthur Ingram of Yorkshire, who sold it to Lionel Cranfield, Earl of Essex. It is not known when or where Edward Greville died.

Richard Lane (c1556-1613)

Richard was a Warwickshire landowner and the son of Nicholas Lane, who lent money to Shakespeare's uncle and sued his father for its recovery. Richard Lane helped John Shakespeare in the litigation over Wilmcote and joined William Shakespeare and Thomas Greene in the tithes dispute of 1611. He married Joan Whitney from Surrey and in 1603 bought **Alveston Manor**. Richard appointed Shakespeare's son-in-law, Hall, as trustee for his children on the 9th July 1613, six days before his nephew John Lane, was sued by Hall's wife Susannah for defamation.

John Lane (1590-1640)

John was the grandson of Nicholas Lane and nephew of Richard. He was a defendant in a slander suit brought by Shakespeare's daughter Susannah in July 1613. He did not appear at the court and was excommunicated. Six years later he was sued by the Star Chamber for riot and for libelling the vicar and alderman. He was also presented by the churchwardens of Stratford to the Church Court as a drunkard. His sister Margaret married John Greene, Shakespeare's kinsman.

The Star Chamber: was an English court of law which sat at the royal Palace of Westminster, from the late 15th century to the mid-17th century (c1641) and was composed of Privy Councillors and common law judges, and of the common law judges, to supplement the judicial activities of the common law courts and in civil and criminal matters. The Star Chamber was established to ensure the fair enforcement of the law or laws against socially and politically prominent people so powerful that ordinary courts would likely hesitate to convict them of their crimes.

Susannah Shakespeare (Hall) 26th May 1583-11th July 1649) –

was the oldest child of William Shakespeare and Anne Hathaway and the older sister of Judith Quiney and Hamnet Shakespeare. Susanna married John Hall, who was a local physician in 1607. They had one daughter, named Elizabeth, in 1608.

Hall's Croft- the home of Shakespeare's daughter Susanna and her husband Dr John Hall: - RHH©

One of Shakespeare's six known signatures and a portrait by an unknown artist of Anne Hathaway

Anne Hathaway's Cottage at nearby Shottery where William courted Anne: - JRH

Shakespeare's children, Susanna, the oldest and twins Hamnet and Judith. One of the twins Hamnet, passed away of unknown causes-possibly the plague at the age of 11 – artist Sofanisba©

In June 1613, John Lane accused Susanna of adultery with Rafe Smith, a 35 year old haberdasher and claimed she had caught venereal disease from Smith. As a notable Puritan of the community, Hall supported the Puritan vicar, Thomas Wilson, against whom Lane would later participate in a riot, and it is possible that Lane's charges had political motives in defaming Susanna. On 15th July the Halls brought a suit for slander against Lane in the Consistory Court in Worcester. Robert Whatcott, who three years later witnessed Shakespeare's will, testified for the Halls, but Lane failed to appear and was found guilty of slander and excommunicated. In 1619 Lane was found guilty of slander again, this time for attacks on the vicar and local aldermen; he was also named in court as a persistent drunkard.

Susannah Shakespeare ('Hall' on her marriage) and a romantic picture of Shakespeare's family

The **manor of Alveston** seems to have been originally coterminous with the parish, with the additions of certain meadow lands in Hampton Lucy and Hatton on the north bank of the Avon: 3 acres of meadow opposite the mill are included in Oswald's grant of 966.

One of the fine stained glass windows at Alveston Manor Hotel showing 'Alveston Manor held by the Church of Worcester under Bishop Oswald in 966.':- JRH©

Sir Robert de Clopton early in the 13th century granted 6 acres in Hampton Meadow to the prior of Worcester, to be held of the king in the **manor of Alveston**, at a rent of 4s. yearly. These and other holdings in Hampton Meadow and under Hatton Hill passed with the site of the manor to the Peers family in the 16th century.

'*Robert de Clopton came no doubt from Clopton near Stratford. He certainly alienated (tr*ansferred ownership of (property rights) to another person or group) *some property at nearby* **Alveston** *early in the 13th century – Lordships, Knighthood and Locality: A study in English Society, C.1180-1280.*

Robert Peers was a wine merchant of Bristol, who, it is said settled at **Alveston** in 1540. He was the son of *Richard Peers of Grimley*, Worcs (d.1521) and the brother of *William Moore*, Prior of Worcester, through whose interest he obtained in 1522 the reversion of the office of Yeoman of the Chamber to the monastery. He is mentioned as bailiff of the manor under the crown in 1546 and died in 1550.

The Peers Coat of Arms – Azure a fesse argent between three pelicans or with three roundels gules on the fesse.

William Moore: From 1518-1535 he was the prior of the Benedictine Priory of St Mary's Worcester.

His journal survives and details his weekly expenses, entertainment and journeys from 1518 to 1535, giving an insight into the life of the head of a large religious house just before the Reformation. 'The Monastery and Cathedral of Worcester' (1866) by John Noake, gives more information about this. William Moore's effigy is said to be behind the main altar in the Cathedral.

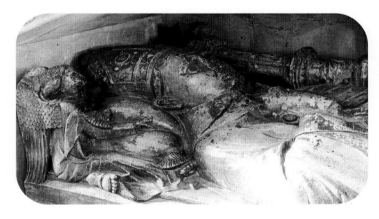

The effigy behind the altar pertaining to be that of William Moore in Worcester Cathedral: - courtesy of the Dean and Chapter of Worcester Cathedral©

In 1534, the Prior, sub prior and thirty seven of the monks subscribed to the oath of the royal supremacy, denying the authority of the pope in England. In 1535, at the age of sixty three, he retired to the manor house of Crowle on a generous pension just before the Dissolution. In 1542 the Prior died in Alveston village close to the original manor house and is in fact not buried in Worcester Cathedral, but at the old church of St James, Alveston. His house which is still standing today is part of *Alveston Lodge*.

Alveston Lodge: - courtesy of Mr Brian Johnson©

After Alveston Manor Hotel this is the second oldest dwelling in the parish. The central part of the house, believed to be early 16th century, was occupied by Prior Moore who was Prior of Worcester from 1518 to 1535. The rear of the house was added in the 18th century and the front added in the 19th.

Prior Moore managed to secure for his brother the ownership of Alveston. At one time he was the guardian of Anne Boleyn. He found time to write a book on fishponds as well as keeping an account of every farthing that he spent.

Moore spent little time at the Priory in Worcester; he spent his time at his various houses at Battenhall, Crowle and Grimley as well as regular visits to London. He carried with him a retinue of some size – *'four gentlemen, ten yeomen, and ten grooms, in addition to a chaplain and monk-steward; he also maintained indoor and outdoor servants that encumbered every large house of the age.'*

****

Twenty years later, Robert's son and heir *Edmund Peers* purchased the **Manor house** and the site of the manor for £576 9s. 2d. from *Ludovic Greville. Edmund Peers* obtained a grant of arms in 1605 and died in 1609. His son *Thomas,* who was a recusant, received livery of the property from the Crown in 1614 and died in 1646. He was followed successively by his son and grandson; both named Thomas, the latter of which died in London in 1722.

Recusancy: *was the state of those who had refused to attend Anglican services, the word coming from the Latin recusare (to refuse or make an objection). It was first used to refer to those who remained loyal to the Roman Catholic Church and did not attend Church of England services, with a 1593 statute determining the penalties against 'Popish recusants'. The 'Recusancy Acts' began in the reign of Elizabeth I and were repealed in 1650 by Oliver Cromwell. They imposed various punishments for those accused such as fines, property confiscation and imprisonment.*

Lieutenant Colonel Newsham Peers, eldest surviving son of Thomas III, succeeded to the estates and died in 1743 of wounds received at Dettingen.

The Battle of Dettingen took place on the 27th June 1743 at Dettingen on the River Main, Germany during the War of the Austrian Succession. The British forces were in alliance with those of Hanover and Hess, and defeated a French army under the command of the duc de Noailles. George II commanded his troops in the battle and marked the last time a British monarch personally led his troops on the field. It was a local man, Colonel Newsham Peers of Alveston, who was the last Colonel to lead his Regiment under fire. Newsham Peers was the Colonel of the Royal Welch Fusiliers at the time of the battle and had been a professional soldier all his life; Peers was mortally wounded in the course of the battle. A memorial to Peers is to be found in Saint James' Old Church, Mill Lane, Alveston, within sight of the manor where he lived. The inscription reads:

To the Memory of the Hon. NEWSHAM PEERS Esq. Colonel of His Majesty's
own Royal Regiment of WELCH FUZILIERS.
He had been a Commission Officer 40 Years
And distinguished Himself in most
Of the Sieges & Battles during the reign
of QUEEN ANNE.
He dyed July 28th 1743 of his Wounds He received
At the battle of DETTINGGEN
And was buried in St Philip Rue's Chapel
Near HANAU in GERMANY.
Regretted by his King lamented by his Country

The memorial, carved in white/grey marble and surmounted by the family arms, is on the north wall of the chancel close to the sanctuary and was placed there by Peers's grieving family.

The inscription gives us a good insight into Peers's military service; he had been commissioned, probably in 1705, into the regiment of his uncle, Colonel Joseph Sabine, the Royal Welch Fusiliers or 23rd Regiment of Foot. He was promoted Lieutenant on 24th June 1707 and was wounded at the battle of Malplaquet on 11th November 1709. Steady promotions followed; to Captain in 1710, to m

Major in 1720 and then to Lieutenant Colonel on Christmas Day 1722 when he became the Commanding Officer of the regiment. Colonel Sabine died on 24th October 1739 and Peers succeeded him as the Regimental Colonel. Newsham Peers would have been in his late fifties at the time of Dettingen; although campaigning life was more comfortable for a senior officer than for a foot soldier there is little doubt that Peers was a hardy soul, capable of withstanding the rigours of life in the field. (*With thanks to the trustees of the Royal Welch Fusiliers Regimental Museum, Caernarvon and to Dr Kevin Mason FMA for this information and a copy of the Colonel's will*).

The monument on Alveston Old Church to the Hon. Newsham Peers: - courtesy of Brian Johnson©

His Will makes for interesting reading and gives us today a fine insight into life in the 18th century.

George II at the Battle of Dettingen by John Wootton

Portrait of Colonel Newsham Peers: - By kind permission of the trustees of the Royal Welch Fusiliers Regimental Museum, Caernarfon© (see colour plate)

The Will of Colonel Newsham Peers is dated 21ˢᵗ June 1732 – 'Will of Newsham Peers, Alveston, Esq.'

Bequests to brothers, Philip and Edmund (of New York), sister Elizabeth.

To friends Lt Gen. Joseph Sabine, John Knight of Gosfield Hall, Essex., Esq., John Marsh, Middle Temple, Richard Marriett, Anscott, Warks., Esq. to Aunt Ann Knight, Gosfield Hall. To kinsman James Newsham, Chadshunt, Warks. Esq.

Gosfield Hall – *was built in 1545 by Sir John Wentworth a member of Cardinal Wolsey's household and hosted Royal visits by Queen Elizabeth I and her grand retinue throughout the middle of the 16ᵗʰ century.*

The day before the Colonel died on the 16ᵗʰ July 1743 after being shot in the throat, he wrote a codicil to his will. (The Colonel after being shot lived for another 27days in much pain and probably would have been unable to eat.)

Copy codicil written in expectation of not surviving wounds: appointing 2 fellow officers Major Roger Lent and Capt. Richard Bendythe as trustees to dispose of personal and military equipment in Germany and at Ghent.

Horses to be sold; English roan gelding with accoutrements to Capt. John Bernard; Double shot pistol to James Newsham; remaining wine to be drunk by Officers of the Regiment; locked chests and trunks to be sent to brother Capt. Philip Peers; two camp tables to Mrs Stupreant in Ghent; servants saddles, bridles and pistols to servant Abraham Banks. Pecuniary bequests to servant William Wessell, surgeons, washerwomen, soldiers who carried him off the field of battle, new shirt to soldier who tore up his for bandages, clothes to servant Wessell.

The **Alveston** property passed by his will to his younger brother Philip, the commander of an East Indiaman, who died at Bombay in 1751. Philip devised it to another brother Edmund (1687-1766), with whose son, Newsham Peers (1726-1803), the male line of the family came to an end. The estate was sold under the will of Newsham Peers to Henry Roberts of Stratford for £39,500 (£1,341,420) in 1810.

* *

By the 20th century the former manor house was then the residence of Lieut Colonel R. H. R. Brocklebank.

Lt Col. Richard Hugh Royds Brocklebank – was the son of Thomas

Brocklebank. He married Charlotte Carissma Blood, the daughter of General Sir Bindon Blood and Charlotte Elizabeth Colvin, on 14th September 1910. They had two sons and one daughter. He died on the 8th May 1965.

He was a member of Magdalen College in Oxford and became a considerable collector of paintings, prints and iznik pottery, as his father had been. His collection included eight paintings by or attributed to Richard Wilson. These were bequeathed to Magdalen College in 1965.

Iznik Pottery – was named after the town in western Anatolia where it was made. It is a decorated ceramic that was produced from the last quarter of the 15th century until the end of the 17th century.

The Ruins of Hadrian's villa, Tivoli – (after) Richard Wilson: - courtesy of Magdalen College, Oxford©

He lived at **Alveston House**, Stratford-upon-Avon. He gained the rank of Lieutenant Colonel in the service of the 9th Queen's Royal Lancers. He was invested as a Companion, Distinguished Service Order (DSO). He held the office of Deputy Lieutenant (DL) and was also a Justice of the Peace.

Col. Brocklebank was the nephew of Ralph Brocklebank of Haughton Hall, Tarporley, Cheshire. The family fortune was based on shipping of Whitehaven and banking.

It is difficult to find all the residents of the old Manor through the years and on various occasions advertisements have appeared with the Manor being rented. One such advertisement appeared in *The Times* for the 26th September 1860:

*Alveston, Warwickshire – To LET, unfurnished at Michaelmas next. **ALVESTON MANOR HOUSE** situated a quarter of a mile from Stratford-upon-Avon, eight miles from Warwick and 10 miles from Leamington. The house is a convenient family residence, with excellent gardens, stables, coach-house, out-buildings &c. With or without an adjoining nine acres of good pasture land. Apply to G, Spoonar Esq., 34 Waterloo Street, Birmingham.'*

In the *Warwick and Warwickshire Advertiser* for the 11th August 1917 in the middle of the First World War is mentioned the following, which links with **Alveston Manor:**

*'Major E. P. B. Morrall, son of Col. And Mrs Morrall, who lived at one time at **Alveston Manor,** was killed in action July 28th. In May he was posted to a battalion of the Border Regiment in France and was acting second in command. His Colonel writes, "His death was a very great loss to the battalion. He made a splendid commander always cheery, most hard working and quite fearless. I feel a keen sense of personal sorrow and loss at his death.'*

He was the only son of Colonel Abel Morrall. In 1888 the family had lived at the manor house at Studley, and in 1992 was shown to be living at the **Alveston Manor House**. The Morralls were among the most important needle manufacturers in Studley at one time.

* *

Chapter Three: The Manor House

The present Alveston Manor Hotel with a view to the front of the hotel: - courtesy of the Alveston Manor Hotel & Adrian Wroth – photographer©

The rear façade of the Alveston Manor Hotel. This was originally the front entrance with a sweeping drive to the front door: - courtesy of the Alveston Manor Hotel & Adrian Wroth – photographer©

The Alveston Manor Hotel is a Grade 11 listed manor house (first listed on the 25th October 1951) by Historic England. The description of the building reads as follows:

The house, now a hotel is dated to c1500, and enlarged in c1600, C17, and C18 with a 19th century restoration and later 20th century restorations and additions. The house has timber framing with brick infill; many panels have decorative brick and tile work with some stucco to the rear; tile roofs with brick stacks.

An early 20th century view of the Alveston Manor Hotel: - courtesy of Mr Andrew Bridges of Hereford©

The same view of the former front entrance to the Manor in December 2016: - JRH©

The house is two storeys. There is a nucleus of 3 gabled bays. One to the left projects, with later flanking wings (one 16th the other late 17th); the outer wings 18th that to the right end project. The entrance, to the left of the centre, has a mid to late 20th century glazed flat-roofed porch; similar entrance to the right end. The windows have late 20th century casements with leaded glazing replacing sashes (recorded 1972); the central 1st-floor Venetian window with leaded glazing. Two c16 century axial stacks with square shafts with fillets and cornices close studding with middle rails and one 17th century stack. The rear has a stucco 3-gable centre with trail and fretwork. There is a large c20th century single-storey flat-roofed addition and corridor to the right.

The lodge at the entrance to what was originally the main entrance drive into the Manor: - JRH©

Interior: entrance hall has 17th century panelling and chamfered beams; the stairs have square newels with finials and splat balusters. Many of the upper rooms were heightened into the roof space in the 18^{h} century panelling. The north-east room of the oldest part shows the original north wall with an old tie beam and close studding (in line with the wall of the main block) now enclosed by the 17^{h} century north-east wing.

The staircase at the Alveston Hotel: - JRH©

The main hall has linenfold panelling, the top panels with reticulated tracery (VCH records 9 panels of C16 linenfold); fireplace with stop-chamfered and 19th century Delft tiles, the overmantel has ten panels in early Renaissance style with high relief heads in roundels, similar panels to two doors.

The 'Blue Lounge' with the magnificent fireplace surrounded by Delft tiles and the heraldry on the windows: - courtesy of the Alveston Manor Hotel& Adrian Wroth-photographer© (see colour plate)

Early view of the present 'Blue Lounge' c1920s: - courtesy of Michael Careless©

The wood panelled reception area at the Alveston Manor Hotel: - JRH

Example of the linenfold panelling: - JRH©

Some of the fine woodcarving over the doors in the 'Blue Lounge': - JRH©

The large room at the end of a short corridor is the Manor Bar Lounge with paired door with linenfold panelling and with a coffered ceiling, and large stone fireplace with armorial bearing over. The rear passage has exposed timber framing and many late 19th century panels recording the history of the house.

The Manor Bar Lounge with its large stone fireplace and armorial bearings: - courtesy of the Alveston Manor Hotel & Adrian Wroth-photographer©

The Manor Bar: - courtesy of the Alveston Manor Hotel & Adrian Wroth – photographer©

The armorial bearing shield over the fireplace: - courtesy of the Alveston Manor Hotel & Adrian Wroth – photographer©

In the panelled 'Blue Lounge' of the hotel is a fine fireplace surrounded by a collection of interesting and charming Delft tiles. The subjects are various showing Aesop's fables and stories from fairy tales and the Greek myths.

The magnificent fireplace in the Alveston Manor Hotel with the collection of Delph tiles

The 'Blue Lounge': courtesy of the Alveston Manor Hotel & Adrian Wroth - photographer©

Some of the Delft tiles in the 'Blue Lounge' at the Alveston Manor Hotel showing scenes from Aesop's Fables: - JRH©

Delftware or Delft pottery which is also known as Delft Blue due to its unique colouration was manufactured around the Dutch city of Delft in the Netherlands from the 16th century.

Delftware is one of the tin-glazed earthenware or *faience* in which a white glaze is applied, which is then decorated with metal oxides. It forms part of the worldwide family of *blue and white pottery*, which was initially developed in the 14th century. Chinese porcelain became in great demand in Europe. Delftware included pottery objects of all descriptions such as plates, ornaments and tiles. The most highly regarded period of production was from about 1640-1740.

Johannes Vermeer's painting of Delft - 1660-1661

The Delft potters made tiles in vast numbers (estimated at eight hundred million) over a period of two hundred years. Many houses still have tiles that were fixed in the 17th and 18th centuries.

Delftware became popular and was widely exported in Europe and even reached China and Japan. The Japanese potters made porcelain versions of Delftware for export to Europe.

Some of the other Delft tiles in the 'Blue Lounge' at Alveston Manor Hotel: -JRH©

Heraldry: The Alveston Manor Hotel has some interesting examples of Heraldic Shields. They are not contemporary with the house, but they complement the Hotel and I have tried to discover more about their origins and design.

Heraldry is a broad term, which encompasses the design, display and study of armorial bearings, together with the study of ceremony, rank and pedigree. Armory, the most familiar branch of heraldry, concerns the design and transmission of the heraldic achievement, which is more commonly known as the coat of arms. This usually consists of a shield, helmet and crest as supporters, and badges, heraldic banners and mottoes.

Although the use of various devices to signify individuals and groups goes back into the mists of time, both the form and use of such devices varied widely and the concept of regular, heraldry designs, constituting the distinguishing features of heraldry, did not develop until the High Middle Ages. The use of helmets when going into battle made it difficult to distinguish and recognise one's commanders in the field when large armies were gathered together for extended periods, necessitating the development of heraldry as a symbolic langue in its own right.

In modern times, heraldry is used by individuals, public and private organisations, corporations, cities, towns and regions to symbolise their heritage, achievements and

aspirations. The Alveston Manor's owners 'Macdonald Alveston' have their own shield which they use to promote and advertise their group:

The logo or crest of the Macdonald Group of Hotels

Here are some of the heraldic shields which are found in the Alveston Manor Hotel and their definitions. The arms are mostly Royal arms and are most attractive.

One of the Heraldic Shields in the 'Blue Lounge – The Royal Arms of George I, II and III until 1801 (from 1714). The fourth quarter (bottom right) is for Hanover- Thanks to A.P.S. de Redman, F.S.A. Scot., Hon. F.H.S., Birmingham City Honorary Armorist.(see colour plates for these Heraldry illustrations).(See colour plate)

*Examples of the splendid heraldry shields in the oak panelled lounge today 'The Blue Lounge': -
The Royal Arms from 1801 to 1816 or from 1816 to 1837. Hanover is moved to the centre with an
Electoral Bonnet (1801 to 1816) and then a Crown for the Kingdom of Hanover 1816-1837. (When
Victoria succeeded to the throne of the United Kingdom but not to the Kingdom of Hanover which
devolved to her uncle.) - JRH© - (Thanks for the research from A.P.S. de Redman, F.S.A. Scot.,
Hon. F.H.S., Birmingham City Honorary Armorist.)*

*The Arms of King William III (William of Orange) and also William and Mary. The shield in the
centre is William's paternal Coat of Nassau*

Red shield with Shamrock – plant badge for Ireland. Blue shield with daffodils – plant badge for Wales (since David Lloyd George disliked the leek). The Blue shield with yellow roses – plant badge for England & Red shield with thistles – plant badge of Scotland: - Thanks to Mr A. P. S. de Redman, F. S. A. Scot., Hon. F.H.S., Birmingham City Honorary Armorist. (see colour plate). The stained glass were placed by Mr W. T. Bird the father of Tony Bird OBE©

Red shield with Fetterlock enclosing a falcon in yellow – the badge of Edmund Langley, fifth son of Edward III, and subsequent Dukes of York (including King Edward IV)-Blue shield with yellow fleur-de-lys for France – Blue shield with yellow rose – England & the Red shield with stylised yellow thistle - Scotland: - courtesy of the Alveston Manor Hotel and thanks to Mr Tony Bird OBE whose father placed these windows at the Manor©

The 'Blue Lounge' – notice the royal coats of arms either side of the entrance to the Cedar Room: -
JRH©

The Heraldic Shields over the fireplace in the 'Blue Lounge' – in ancient times the shield or coat of
arms of the visiting guest and his family were painted here: - courtesy of the Alveston Manor Hotel &
Adrian Wroth – photographer©

The splendid carved Oak door in the 'Blue Lounge' with some of the finely carved faces - said to be 'The Twelve Apostles' - JRH©

Details from the carved oak doors in the 'Blue Lounge': - courtesy of the Alveston Manor Hotel &
Adrian Wroth – photographer©

An early view of the Alveston c1910: - courtesy of Michael Careless©

Alveston Manor with its fine stack of chimneys, an early photograph of the late 1890s or early twentieth century: - courtesy of Michael Careless©

Both of the 16th century chimney stacks have rows of four brick square shafts with facial pilasters. There is also a stack of two square shafts of the 17th century over the west side of the older south-west wing.

The front entrance and the splendid chimney stacks on the present Alveston Manor Hotel: - courtesy of the Alveston Manor Hotel & Adrian Wroth – photographer©

The Alveston Manor Hotel: - courtesy of the Macdonald Alveston Manor Hotel & Adrian Wroth – photographer©

The rear of the Alveston Manor Hotel: - courtesy of the Alveston Manor Hotel & Adrian Wroth – photographer©

The figure of William Shakespeare in front of the Alveston Manor Hotel: - JRH

The Manor Bar: - courtesy of the Alveston Manor Hotel & Adrian Wroth – photographer©

The Delft tiles in the splendid fireplace in the 'Blue Lounge': - courtesy of the Alveston Manor Hotel©

The 'Blue Lounge' with the fine collection of Delft tiles in the fireplace: - courtesy of the Alveston Manor Hotel and Adrian Wroth - photographer©

A selection of the Delft tiles featuring 'Aesop's Fables' in the 'Blue Lounge': - courtesy of the Alveston Manor Hotel & photograph by JRH©

An heraldic lion from the mantelpiece in the 'Blue Lounge': - courtesy of the Alveston Manor Hotel
& Adrian Wroth – photographer©

One of the bedrooms in the stable block of the Alveston Manor Hotel: - courtesy of the Alveston Manor Hotel & Adrian Wroth – photographer©

One of the fine bedrooms at the Alveston Manor Hotel: - courtesy of the Alveston Manor & Adrian Wroth – photographer©

The Swimming Pool at the Alveston Manor Hotel Spa: - courtesy of Alveston Manor Hotel &
Adrian Wroth – photographer©

The Gym as part of the Alveston Manor Hotel Spa: - courtesy of the Alveston Manor Hotel & Adrian Wroth – photographer©

St Anthony the Great, father of Christian Monasticism and an early anchorite

Colonel Newsham Peers: - by kind permission of the trustees of the Royal Welch Fusiliers
Regimental Museum, Caernarfon©

THE BUILDING OF ALVESTON MANOR BY THE MONKS.

ALVESTON MANOR HELD BY THE CHURCH OF WORCESTER UNDER BISHOP OSWALD IN 966

Two of the fine stained glass windows at Alveston Manor Hotel showing the history of the manor of Alveston: - courtesy of the Alveston Manor Hotel© Photograph – JRH©

BISHOP WULFSTAN MAINTAINS HIS TITLE TO THE
MANOR BEFORE QUEEN MATILDA IN 1089.

One of the stained glass panels from the Alveston Manor Hotel featuring Bishop Wulfstan and
Queen Elizabeth I: - courtesy of the Alveston Manor Hotel.(c) Photograph – JRH©

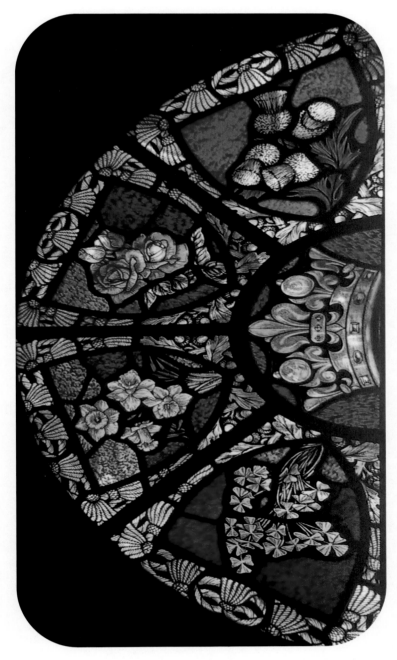

Red shield with Shamrock – plant badge for Ireland. Blue shield with daffodils – plant badge for Wales (since David Lloyd George disliked the leek). The Blue shield with yellow roses – plant badge for England & Red shield with thistles – plant badge of Scotland: - Thanks to Mr A. P. S. de Redman, F. S. A. Scot., Hon. F.H.S., Birmingham City Honorary Armorist. Photograph – JRH© Thanks to Mr Tony Bird OBE whose father Mr W.T. Bird placed these windows when the family owned the Manor.

Red shield with Fetterlock enclosing a falcon in yellow – the badge of Edmund Langley, fifth son of Edward III, and subsequent Dukes of York (including King Edward IV)-Blue shield with yellow fleur-de-lys for France – Blue shield with yellow rose – England & the Red shield with stylised yellow thistle – Scotland. Photograph - JRH©

*One of the splendid heraldry shields at Alveston Manor – The Royal Arms of George I, II
and III until 1801 (from 1714). The fourth quarter is for Hanover: - JRH©*

One of the stained glass windows showing scenes from Shakespeare's 'Romeo and Juliet': -
courtesy of the Alveston Manor Hotel & Adrian Wroth – photographer©

One of the stained glass windows showing scenes from Shakespeare plays: - courtesy of the Alveston Manor Hotel & Adrian Wroth – photographer©

The Royal Shakespeare Theatre - Stratford-upon-Avon: - JRH©

The Gower Monument to William Shakespeare presented to the town of Stratford-upon-Avon in 1888 by Lord Ronald Gower. The work was executed in Paris and took 12 years to complete: -
JRH©

The bronze figures of Falstaff, Hamlet, Henry V and Lady Macbeth surrounding the Gower Monument: - JRH©

The Royal Shakespeare Theatre Stratford: - courtesy of the Royal Shakespeare Theatre RSC &
photograph by Stewart Hemley©

The Royal Shakespeare Theatre Stratford: - courtesy of the Royal Shakespeare Theatre RSC© &
photograph by Peter Cook© RSC

Shakespeare's Schoolroom at the Edward VIth Grammar School in Stratford-upon-Avon: - courtesy of Mr Tony Bird OBE

Chapter Four: The Gardens

To see how the gardens have been laid out over the centuries at Alveston Manor has not been easy. There is no evidence of the early formal gardens which must have existed in the distant past and no engravings or drawings of them either. The drawing of the early 19th century shows that the gardens were laid out with grass and with tree avenues. The one known as the 'Monks Walk' has now disappeared when the house became a hotel and when the Forte Hotel group took over and made a lot of changes to the gardens and grounds.

An early 19th century view of the Alveston Manor showing the avenues and the gazebo in situ: - courtesy of the Shakespeare Birthplace Trust Archives©

One interesting feature was the 18th century gazebo or summer house which stood at the end of the gardens but now after road changes is isolated on a road traffic island just outside the grounds of the hotel.

The 18th century Gazebo: - JRH©

This is an example of an early 18th century gazebo which was part of the original gardens of the Alveston Manor Hotel. It was probably Georgian in period (1714-1836).

A photograph of the Alveston Gazebo during a flood, before it was separated from the Hotel gardens by a road: - courtesy of Mr Anthony Bird OBE©

A Gazebo is in fact a pavilion type of structure, sometimes octagonal or turret-shaped, often built as a feature of a garden or park. They are often free-standing as in the Alveston example or attached to the garden wall. They provide shelter, shade and an ornamental feature in the garden, a place to rest, or to enjoy a quiet moment of personal time.

Gazebos can include pavilions, kiosks, alhambras, belvederes, follies, pergolas and also rotundas. They are popular in warm and sunny climates, and often feature in the literature of China and Persia. Some other examples in England can be found at such locations as Montecute House in Somerset or at Elton on the Hill in Nottinghamshire.

The Gazebo at Montecute House in Somerset and the tree house gazebo at Pitchford Hall in Shropshire

The Eyton on Severn Banqueting House (Gazebo) built around 1595 by the master mason Walter Hancock for Sir Francis Newport's Eyton Hall.) – A local myth states that Shakespeare between the ages of 18-21 was a personal tutor to the Newport family here at Eyton: - JRH©

The gardens have obviously changed over the centuries as fashions have changed. Today the gardens both to the front and the rear of the present hotel are laid to grass and some small shrub beds.

The gardens to the front of the present hotel, laid out to shrubs and small trees and lawn. You can get an idea of the length of the gardens by the brick wall in the distance signifying what were once the kitchen gardens of the Manor. Today there is a modern housing development: - JRH

The modern entrance with a few planted shrubs and the statue of Shakespeare in a small yew hedge garden enclosure to the front of the Hotel: courtesy of the Alveston Manor Hotel & Adrian Wroth – photographer©

Alveston Manor Hotel from the gardens and the famous Cedar of Lebanon: - JRH©

*The rear gardens of the present Alveston Manor Hotel: - courtesy of the Alveston Manor Hotel &
Adrian Wroth – photographer©*

The famous Cedar of Lebanon or 'Kissing Tree' in the gardens of Alveston Manor: - JRH

The famous Cedar of Lebanon in the gardens of Alveston Manor is said to be one of the
oldest examples of this species of tree in England. It is said to be the site of where William

Shakespeare experienced his first kiss and where the first production of *'A MidsummerNight's Dream'* was performed.

One of the stained glass windows from the hotel depicting a scene from 'Romeo and Juliet.': - courtesy of the Alveston Manor Hotel & Adrian Wroth – photographer©

Other Shakespeare plays were performed here in the open air; here is a programme for *'Twelfth Night.'*

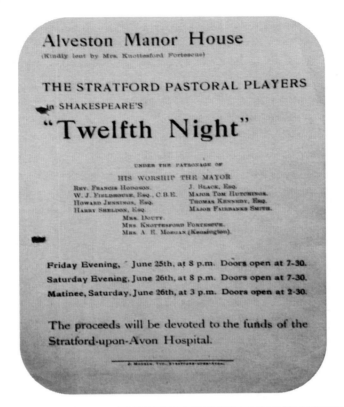

A performance at the Alveston in the c1920/30s: - courtesy of the Shakespeare Birthplace Trust Archives©

The Cedar of Lebanon:

The *Cedrus libani* is a species of the Cedar which is native to the mountains of Mediterranean regions and the Lebanon Cedar has been widely planted as an ornamental tree in many parks and gardens. It is often used by landscape artists as part of their plans for great country houses and the layout of extensive gardens.

It is unknown when the first cedar of Lebanon was planted in Britain, but it dates at least to 1664 and so a little too late for Shakespeare's time (1564-1616), as mentioned in '*Sylva, or A Discourse of Forest-Trees and the Propagation of Timber.* However, the story of the 'kissing tree' is still a fine touch even though it is more than likely a myth.

It is not known when the first cedar tree of Lebanon was planted in Britain, but it dates from at least 1664, when it was mentioned in *Sylva, or A Discourse of Forest-Trees and the Propagation of Timber.*

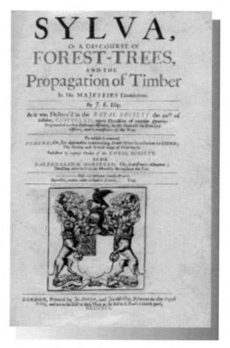

The title page to the first edition of 1664

Sylva, or A Discourse of Forest-Trees and the Propagation of Timber in His Majesty's Dominions by the English writer John Evelyn was first presented in 1662 as a paper to the Royal Society. It was published as a book two years later in 1664, and is recognised as one of the most influential texts on forestry ever published.

The tree is known among *arborists* for its tendency to drop branches without warning, and the use of wire bracing or lopping is common to reduce this risk.

The Cedar at Alveston was often used for a background for plays and other events, and the staff would have had to place props to ensure the branches were secure.

This majestic, slow-growing, long-living tree has long been a symbol of immortality and strength. It is mentioned many times in the Bible, and its wood is thought to have been used to build King Solomon's temple.

A drawing of what King Solomon's Temple may have looked like in Jerusalem

The Cedar of Lebanon's natural habitat is found in Syria, the Taurus Mountains in Turkey and Mount Lebanon. As the name suggests, it is closely associated with Lebanon – so much so, that its distinctive outline appears on the Lebanese flag.

The Lebanese flag with the famous 'Cedar of Lebanon' at its centre

The presence and position of the Cedar in the middle of the flag is directly inspired by the mountains of Lebanese cedar *(Cedrus libani)*. The Cedar is a symbol of holiness, eternity and peace. As an emblem of longevity, the cedar of Lebanon has its origin in many Biblical references; in fact it is mentioned seventy-seven times.

For the Lebanese, the cedar is a symbol of hope, freedom and memory. In 1920, in a text of the proclamation of the State of Greater Lebanon, it was said: *'an evergreen cedar is like a young nation despite a cruel past. Although oppressed, never conquered, the cedar is its rallying. By the union, it will break all attacks.'*

The white colour on the flag represents the snow as a symbol of purity and peace. The two red stripes refer to the Lebanese blood shed to preserve the country against the successive invaders.

For the first 40 years of its life the Cedar of Lebanon grows in a conical shape, before developing its distinctive level foliage plates. During the eighteenth century it became very fashionable to plant them in the gardens of large estates and still today it is a popular tree for parks.

In connection with Shakespeare I recently came across this chair which was made from the wood of the Mulberry tree which once stood in Shakespeare's garden in Stratford.

1862 – made for Frederick Cosens with wood from the Old Mulberry Tree now growing in Shakespeare's Great Garden at Stratford-upon-Avon: - courtesy of Mr Anthony Bird OBE©

The Old Coach House:

The Old Coach house or stables was rebuilt in 1951 after being in threat of demolition. The building was rebuilt in the Queen Anne Style and the sundial put back in pride of place. The old barn named after Henry VIII was demolished and today the site is covered over by other buildings.

The Coach House in the gardens of Alveston Manor with the interesting sundial: - JRH©

Early postcard of the Coach House at the Alveston Manor Hotel

*Bedrooms in the Coach House: - courtesy of the Alveston Manor Hotel & Adrian Wroth –
photographer© (see colour plate)*

Chapter Five: The Past Hotel

*Early photograph of the Alveston Manor: while still a family home with a tennis court in the garden -
courtesy of Tony Bird OBE©*

Alveston Manor was purchased by William Bird and family in1938 from the Fortescue
family for £20,000 and after the sale was agreed they moved in. It was, however, not long
after this time that War was declared and the house was requisitioned by the War Office
for use by the Canadian Army.

*One of several early wartime emblems' of the Canadian Army and Air Force who were both
connected with the Alveston Manor during World War II*

ALVESTON MANOR,
STRATFORD-ON-AVON.

TO BE LET ON A LEASE.
UNFURNISHED.

The above is a beautiful old-world Manor House—15th Century—stands in well-timbered and attractive grounds—about 16 Acres—and is 121 feet above Sea Level.

Eleven Bed Rooms and Dressing Rooms, Billiard Room, fine Lounge Hall. Stabling for 6, and Lodge. Motor House. Boat House, and three Cottages.

FRONT VIEW WITH CONSERVATORY ENTRANCE.

In the centre of the Warwickshire Hunt, ¼-mile from old historical town, with stations on G.W.R. and G.C.R. **And** within an easy run of Warwick, Leamington, Alcester, Coventry, Birmingham, and West of England, and 2¼ hours by train from London. **Church,** P. & T. O. within ½-a-mile. **In very** pretty rural district, with walks and drives in all directions. **In** particularly good Sporting and Social district, **Gravel** Soil, healthy and bracing air.

SPORTING.—First-rate Hunting with Warwickshire Fox-hounds (5 days a week), also with North Cotswold Pack.

GOLF LINKS near. Boating, Fishing in the charming River Avon within 3 minutes' walk of the House.

The Catalogue for the letting of part of the Alveston Manor Park in c1934: - courtesy of Mr Anthony Bird OBE©

This delightful old-world Residence is in capital Decorative and Structural Repair, and is a charming and rambling low, many-gabled Country House.

It stands well away from roads in a secluded position, quite free from dust. Faces South-East, and is approached by a good Carriage Drive, with Lodge at entrance, and contains—

GROUND FLOOR.

Conservatory Entrance, Spacious Hall (Lounge about 34' × 19'), with fine open Dog-Grate, and French Casements leading to Garden, and with an Ante-room for writing.

DINING ROOM about 17' square, exclusive of Sideboard Recess, communicating with Library about 20' × 13' 6".

MORNING ROOM 15' × 13', facing S.E., communicating with a fine lofty BILLIARD ROOM about 28' × 19', exclusive of square Bay. Lavatory and W.C. adjoining.

THE DOMESTIC OFFICES are conveniently arranged on the same level, and include Back Hall, Butler's Pantry (h. & c.), spacious Kitchen with Eagle Range, Scullery (h. & c.), Servants' Hall, good Larder and Game Larder. Wine Cellars. Outside Boot and Knife House and Servants' W.C.

FIRST FLOOR

approached by principal and secondary Staircase to DRAWING ROOM, 29' × 17', with S.E. and N.W. Windows, with domed ceiling.

BEST BEDROOM about 18' 6" × 15', with Dressing Room.

LARGE BEDROOM about 28' × 18', with square Bay.

There are also 7 other Bedrooms, two communicating with Dressing Rooms.

BATH ROOM, fitted with hot and cold water and Lavatory Basin (h. & c.), Heated Linen Cupboard, Lavatory with Sink (h. & c.) and draw-off Tap.

SECOND FLOOR.

Two Bedrooms, Box and Tank Rooms.

THE INTERNAL fitments of House comprise of Oak Panelling, many quaint and useful Cupboards, Antique Staircases, &c.

THIS RESIDENCE would appeal strongly to lovers of Ancient Houses.

Telephones, Gas, and Companies' Water laid on.

SANITATION excellent—Cesspool system.

STABLING in character with the House, is in excellent order, and comprises of—
3 Loose Boxes, 3 Good Stalls and loft over. Large Harness Room, with small Range and Boiler. Coach house for four Carriages.

MOTOR HOUSE for two Cars. Store House, large paved Barn (used and fitted for an extra Coach-house). Cow Yard and Sheds.

BEAUTIFUL OLD-WORLD GROUNDS

are secluded and well-timbered and shrubbed.

Capital Croquet and Tennis Lawns.

Productive walled-in Kitchen Garden, about an acre, and Fish Pond.

Well-stocked Orchard. Lean-to Greenhouse and Frames.

Range of Coal Houses, Loose Box, Men's W.C., and well-timbered, Park-like Meadow of about 10 Acres.

In all about 16 Acres.

RENT: £200 A YEAR.
TO BE LET ON LEASE: 7 or 14 YEARS.
Or Rent without the Park and Three Cottages £150 a year.

BACK VIEW.

At the end of the war years the Canadian army left and the family wished to return to their home. Unfortunately the house had been left in a terrible state and a complete renovation was needed. The local council at this time had seen the condition of the manor and proposed to have it demolished but thankfully this decision was overturned by Mr Tom Bird (W.T. Bird).

World War II

As well as some billeting at the Alveston Manor, the Canadian armed forces also had a contingent of the Royal Canadian Air Force based at nearby Wellesbourne Mountford. The Stratford-upon-Avon cemetery contains 137 WW2 burials (most forming a war graves plot), of which 97 are of Canadian airmen.

It has been difficult to discover which branches of the Canadian Air Force and army were stationed at the Alveston during the war, due to restrictions of information but thanks to the Shakespeare Birthplace Trust Archives, a local history pamphlet gives us some information:

'The Canadian Salvation Army established a Forces Club at the Alveston Manor Hotel. During the course of the war, 20,700 Canadian servicemen and women stayed there. Many of these were aircrews from the No.22 O stationed operational Training Wing based at Wellesbourne and Atherstone.' (N. Fogg – Stratford: A Town at War 1914-1945,p.97)

The cemetery on Evesham Road was a special area for Commonwealth servicemen who had lost their lives. These were predominantly air crews.

In Holy Trinity Church, where Shakespeare is buried is a memorial plaque to the brave airmen of the RAF who died in World War 2.

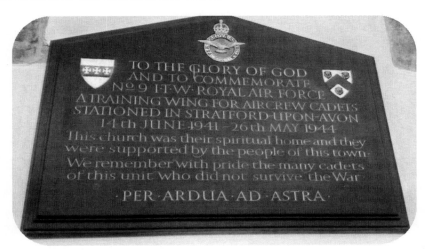

The plaque in Holy Trinity Church – 'To the Glory of God and to Commemorate No9 I.T.W. Royal Air Force. A training wing for the aircrew cadets stationed in Stratford-Upon-Avon 14th June 1941 – 26th May 1944: -JRH©

David Warner in 'WW2 People's War' writes of his memories living close by the Alveston when as a boy he remembers:

'Although I know of no bombs landing on Stratford town in the war, we did have our moments of drama and indeed tragedy. The tragedy occurred in 1943 when a Wellington bomber with engine failure crashed in a field behind our cottage and bordering Kissing Tree Lane.

Merlin-engined Wellington Mark II bomber

My mother had the radio on, and heard nothing of the five aircrew hurtling past her chimney, on their wounded way down, staying with their plane to avoid the village. But our next door neighbour, Doris Pitcher, had heard, seeing the plunging blur of throttled noise. Clad in her wrap-round apron and fluffy slippers she sprinted unevenly over the furrows, strode amongst the triangles of Perspex, the stubs of propellers and the smoking dead engine, to drag the airmen out. If brave women's will have saved them, they would have lived. But those crew members not dead died on the way to the hospital base a mile away. For weeks the village children picked and ferreted amongst the wreckage, seeking Perspex glass to cut and shape with knives into badges, toys and love-rings. On board three of the crew had been young Canadians from the training unit at Wellesbourne. The plane was called 'Queenie', the crew from Saskatchewan, piloted by Light Sergeant James, aged 19. Major Parkes from the village wrote to his parents to tell them what a heroic sacrifice had been made and how proud they should be of the crew of HF632. Two RAF aircrew also perished on the plane.'

* *

The Bird family after the war found the garden in ruins, with slit trenches having been dug over the lawns, and rubbish was piled high by the kitchen area. The roof of the house and the ancient chimneys needed urgent repairs. There had obviously been no maintenance during the War years and a major effort would now be needed to repair the damage. Mr Tony Bird wrote:

'In spite of having a team of bricklayers working on Alveston Manor to restore it, my father who worked with his men seven days a week at his main business brought most of the workmen from his other business on the Birmingham Road to Alveston Manor at weekends to get the job done as quickly as possible. It was a real team effort.'

Mr Bird was allocated a team of German prisoners of war who were stationed at Stratford Racecourse to clear the gardens and to restore them as much as possible, as well as working on the house. About 20 years ago Tony Bird the son of Tom, received a telephone call from the manager of the *Dirty Duck* in the town, that he had a German staying who wished to meet Mr Bird. Tony drove down to the *Dirty Duck* and met this man who turned out to be the sergeant who had been in charge of the work party at the Alveston Manor. He proudly showed Tony Bird the Saville Row suit that Tony's father had given him during the time he was at the Manor – he told of how he himself and his German colleagues had been treated with great kindness which was at this time very much appreciated and they had great respect for Tony's father. The stitching in the suit was absolutely perfect which says something for Saville Row's quality!

Mr John Wiggington, a local antique dealer, had also worked on the renovations and sold back to Mr Bird, a quantity of linenfold panelling, which he originally had bought from the previous owner the Rev. Fortescue, and kept in store for the previous 10 years unable to find a client to buy it. This panelling matched the remnants of the panelling still remaining after the war in the main hall, and so was carefully restored to its original position.

The splendid linenfold panelling in the 'Blue Lounge' and entrance lobby of the Alveston Manor: - courtesy of the Alveston Hotel & Adrian Wroth - photographer©

The Main Lounge – 'The Gold Room' - when the Hotel was being run by the Bird Family. This splendid dining table is still owned by the Bird family and is at Upper Billesley: - courtesy of Mr Anthony Bird OBE©

The fine Tudor dining table in 2016 (not from the Welcombe) plus some of the original chairs from the Welcombe Hotel (now at Upper Billesley): - courtesy of Mr Anthony Bird OBE©

The Welcombe Hotel near Stratford-upon-Avon (see John Hodges's book 'Welcombe House – The Story of a Victorian Calendar House')- JRH©

Finely carved chairs from Welcombe House, the former home of Sir Otto and Lady Caroline Trevelyan: - courtesy of Mr Anthony Bird OBE©

The finely carved leg of the Tudor Bird family dining table

After the war, wood was still being rationed to build much needed houses for the returning soldiers. Mr Bird had been building houses with reclaimed materials and was a major UK buyer of army surplus materials, transport and equipment. The oak from tank transporter floors proved to be of great help in the renovation of the house.

The garden wall at the back of the manor was first of all demolished and the bricks were to be reused in refurbishing the main house. Mr Bird who was a boy of about 9 years of age and his brother Brian were given half a crown for every 1000 bricks they cleaned. This was their pocket money and they worked every hour they were not at school cleaning Tudor bricks.

Tony, May, Tom and Brian Bird c1950: - courtesy of Mr Anthony Bird OBE©

The wood needed for the repairs of both the front façade and the back was taken from tank transporters. Wood was in short supply, but hundreds of surplus war transporters were bought up by Mr Bird. The bonus was that they had Irish Bog Oak flooring which had to be exceedingly strong and durable to carry the weight of the army tanks. It was ideal for the purpose of the renovation for making floorboards, window frames and oak beams. The tyres on the axles were sold to trailer makers while the surplus steel frames went for scrap.

The splendid effect of the timbering and brickwork can still be appreciated today in the present Alveston Manor Hotel. Most of the oak facia timbering was the Irish Bog Oak which replaced the rotten beams of the former house.

The rear and front façade of the modern day Alveston Manor Hotel: - courtesy of the Alveston Manor Hotel & photographs by Adrian Wroth & JRH©

Tom Bird replaced the dilapidated conservatory/loggia on the back of the house with the existing brick loggia with a glass roof and made it the entrance to the house. The chimneys also needed urgent work, and it can be noted that some of them are slightly off centre. The reason could have been according to Mr Bird, that Mr Bird senior was teetotal and did not approve of his workmen drinking- but the workmen were known at lunchtime to sneak across the road to the *Swan's Nest* for a pint or so and then return to the Manor, slightly the worse for wear. Tony Bird says this is the reason the brickwork on the chimneys is not exactly straight!

The new loggia and the glass roof added to the rear of the Manor: - courtesy of Mr Anthony Bird OBE©

The loggia in 2017: - JRH©

The interior of the loggia in 2017: - courtesy of the Alveston Manor Hotel & Adrian Wroth – photographer©

The Rollins family's bricklaying team was employed to help with the renovations to the outside of the Manor house. A little later the Manor was turned into one of the largest and finest hotels in Stratford and this was the dream of Mr William Bird's wife May.

It was May Bird who according to her son Anthony furnished the interiors of the new hotel with antiques from the sale of the numerous country houses which had been forced to sell up due to the severe taxation regime of the post-war governments:

'My mother of course did all the interior decorations and bought all the carpets of the finest hotel quality from Selfridges in London. She went to every country house sale in the district and bought top quality antique furniture. The one sale I was told about was at the Welcombe House where my mother bought a great deal of furniture and its famous dining table and also furniture from Clifford Manor, the home of Mr Reese-Moggs who was the editor of The Times. One of his family, Jacob Reese-Moggs, is currently a Conservative MP in a Devon Constituency. My mother bought a large number of Chippendale chairs (and other fine furniture), which she installed around the restaurant dining tables. The tables were made by a carpentry firm belonging to Dick Tracy which my father took over and John Baldwin was a young apprentice at the time and helped to make some of the tables. John has only recently retired from the Bird Group after over 60 years' service.'

Clifford Manor is at one end of the main street of a village not far from Stratford-upon-Avon. There was a timber-framed house of the 15th or 16th century on the site and remodelled in 1903-9, but this building was badly damaged in a fire in 1918. Edwin Lutyens was called in to repair the house, and he and Gertrude Jekyll are also said to have been responsible for the gardens.

Other carpenters who worked for the Bird family business were also brought in to carry out the important renovation and conversion work in the newly planned hotel.

One of the splendid brick chimneys at the Alveston Manor: - JRH©

As well as the renovation to the house and gardens, the Queen Anne stables were converted into three ground floor flats and bedrooms above to link with the main house as additional bedrooms. The new flats were some of the early examples of ensuite.

Tony Bird growing up at the Manor had his own flat in the roof space of the stable block, with a sitting room and bedroom. He put the floor in himself with wood which had been used to make beer barrels.

At one time the two ground floor apartments were occupied by Rudolf Nureyev and Margot Fonteyn. Laurence Olivier often stayed at the Manor and knew the Bird family well.

Rudolf Nureyev & Margot Fonteyn

Lawrence Olivier

The Stable Block in 2017: - JRH©

The present stable block and one of the stable block bedrooms at the Alveston Manor Hotel: - courtesy of the Alveston Manor Hotel & Adrian Wroth – photographer©

The new hotel venture proved very successful and was eventually sold to the Forte Group for c £100,000 as Tony's mother had suffered a heart attack and Tom Bird bought *Wilmcote Manor* to take her away from the stress of running a large hotel. Some years later the Bird Group tried to buy back the hotel for an estimated £8,000,000 but were unsuccessful, The present value is probably in the range of £20,000,000.

Tom Bird employed Donald Brooks of Birmingham to design and manufacture the stained glass at the Alveston. The one set shows Henry VII, Henry VIII and his son

Edward VI. This is in the present hotel dining room and can be seen here just after the dining room had been created for the new hotel.

The dining room at the Alveston with the stained glass windows on the left of the picture& the fine dining chairs: - courtesy of Mr Tony Bird OBE©

Another view of the dining room at the Alveston Manor: - courtesy of Mr Tony Bird OBE©

Donald Brooks's stained glass window portraying Henry VII and Henry VIII: - courtesy of the Alveston Manor Hotel and JRH©

The stained glass panel by Donald Brooks of Birmingham showing Edward VI: - JRH© Thanks to Mr Tony Bird OBE whose father had these windows placed at the Alveston Manor.

Donald Brooks's company also made the splendid stained glass window panels in the hotel which show the history of Alveston Manor. Donald Brooks was an outstanding artist and after his company was bombed in the Blitz, Tom Bird helped him back on his feet by giving him the Alveston Manor work and a great deal more on other projects.

The Building of the Monastery by the Monks of Worcester and Alveston Manor held by the Church of Worcester under Bishop Oswald in 966: - JRH©

Bishop Wulfstan maintains his title to the Manor before Queen Matilda in 1089 & Monks of Worcester lay their petition to the rights of the Manor before Henry III in 1255. These windows were placed by Mr Tony Bird's father Mr W.T. Bird when the family owned the Manor.

Queen Elizabeth being petitioned on behalf of the Manor and Mr William Thomas Bird restoring the Manor: - JRH© & thanks to Alveston Manor Hotel (see colour plates)

The view of the Kitchens in the early 1950s: - courtesy of Mr Tony Bird OBE©

One of the bedrooms in the Alveston Manor Hotel c1950s: - courtesy of Mr Tony Bird OBE©

Bedroom in the early Alveston Manor Hotel- note the fine windows built and fitted by the carpenters of the Bird Company: - courtesy of Mr Anthony Bird OBE©

After the end of World War Two, there was an ancient monastic fish pond in the garden of the Alveston linked by a tunnel to the River Avon. This was later filled in by the Forte Group when they took over the hotel. There was also a beautiful avenue alongside the garden entitled 'The Monks Walk' with ancient yew trees on one side and Cob trees on the other. This ancient and historic walk was levelled by the new hotel group, a tragedy that would surely not have been allowed today. At the end of the walk was a shady arbour, long since gone, and now in its place a car park and land sold for building. This walk and arbour is mentioned in a commentary by Mrs Kemble describing the beauty and charm of Alveston Manor in 1890.

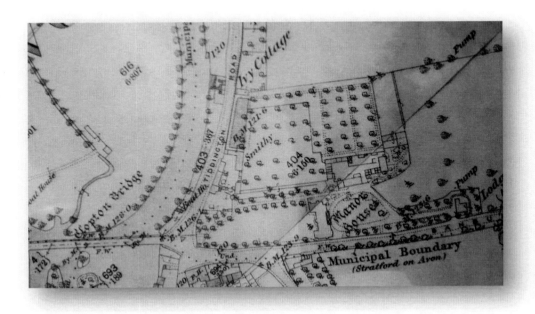

The OS first edition 25 inch map of Alveston Manor for 1885 which shows the Manor House the fish pond and the Monks Walk: - courtesy of the Shakespeare Birthplace Trust Archives©

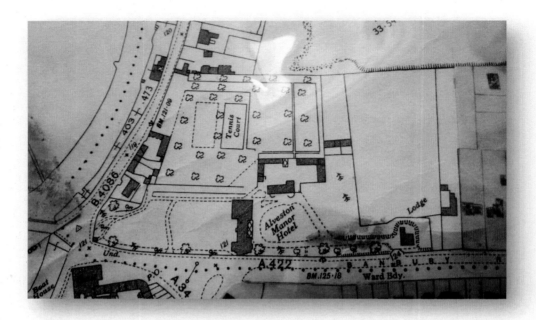

The 1938 25 inch OS Map showing Alveston Manor at the time when the Bird family bought the hotel from the Fortescue's: - courtesy of the Shakespeare Birthplace Trust Archives©

Behind the Queen Anne Stables, the Coach House was at one time an ancient barn, called King Henry VIII barn. This was demolished in the 1950s.

It was said at one time that the gardens at Alveston Manor were the same length and width as Worcester Cathedral. This is probably correct with the monastery at Worcester owning the land and the manor at one time.

The nave of Worcester Cathedral said to be the same length as the gardens of Alveston Manor: - courtesy of the Dean and Chapter of Worcester Cathedral©

An early postcard photograph of the Queen Anne stable block which was converted into ground floor flats and upstairs bedrooms to supplement the hotel: - courtesy of Michael Careless©

The Bird family were an amazing unit and I feel it is well worth writing about their incredible development and their influence not only on the town of Stratford but worldwide.

The Bird Group

The Bird Group was founded in 1912 by W. T. (Tom) Bird, and has a long and interesting history.

At the age of 3, Tom Bird underwent an operation to remove one of his lungs, the first operation ever to remove a lung at the Queen Elizabeth Hospital. This was a major operation taking place before the First World War. He remained in hospital until he was 10 and out of concern for the fate of this child, the doctors and nurses clubbed together to buy him a handcart and gave him £5. They thought then he had the personality and character to get a living and selling firewood from door to door was a good start. They warned him that he should never drink or smoke or he would not live much past his 20th year. He was also told that he must not have any children, as they could have serious health problems. Tom abided by the former advice but ignored the latter and was the father of five children.

Concerning selling firewood he had other ideas and took a pitch in Birmingham's Bull Ring Market – the local barrow boys were not too happy with this young upstart who was very successful and they threw him out a few times. He soon, through hard work and determination gained the confidence and respect of his fellow traders and by the age of 18 was head of a small trading empire, owning most of the pitches in the Bull Ring and market areas of Birmingham and employing a team of over 60 Birmingham barrow boys.

Tom Bird now had 60 men working for him and decided to divert his energies into other areas and his chosen choice was into the motor business. The motor vehicle was the wonder of the age and he owned one of Birmingham Market's first diesel trucks which he used to collect fruit and vegetables from Covent Garden. Several years later he moved to Stratford-upon-Avon and founded the *Birds Commercial Motors* achieving national leadership in selling second-hand buses purchased from municipal bus companies such as Birmingham, London, Manchester and Glasgow and also ex-military war surplus trucks, tanks and transporters from the Ministry of Defence and other vehicles from large transport companies.

In the early days of his diversification into the motor business, he turned the unsaleable vehicles and equipment into a scrap processing business. In 1938 just before the outbreak of WW2, Tom won his first important contract. It was to dismantle the tramway system of Weston super Mare. Equipped with one of those celebrated bull-nosed Morris cars with the roof cut off to accommodate his two gas bottles, a sledgehammer and a set of jacks and four men, he completed the job so efficiently that the following year he was engaged to demolish the town's gasworks. This was the start of Tom Bird in another business – demolition.

Mr W. T. (Tom) Bird:-courtesy of the Bird family©

With the outbreak of war, Tom was not regarded as fit enough to sign up to fight; he only had one lung so was not considered for military service. So he set about cleaning up the mess left by Hitler's bombers. Under Government contract he removed rubble and cleared the bomb sites of twisted metal in the cities of Coventry and Birmingham helping to get the factories back into production, sometimes when the bombing was still going on. He had a team of over 100 men and they were kept busy on a 24 hour basis. He also owned and operated a brickworks at the time, so with the Blitz, his services were in high demand.

1924 Morris bull-nosed Oxford

When the war was over, he expanded into dealing in ex-government surplus supplies, processing scrap and trading in second-hand buses.

In the 1960s, all three brothers were in the company with their father and, in order to find niches for themselves, they gradually steered the company into the reclamation sector in a serious manner. They travelled to the United States where the American scrap business was just starting to modernise, where there were ground breaking ideas in scrap processing machinery, some large enough to crush a whole car or shear a railway truck into small pieces ready for re-melting.

Giant Baling Press at Bird Group's plant in Llanelly & the world's first car crusher as used in the film 'Goldfinger'. The Bird Group operated a fleet of these in the UK and Europe: courtesy of Tony Bird OBE©

When he died in 1973 of pneumonia while on a business trip to America at the age of 72, none of the doctors who had tended him as a child would have believed it possible that he had brought up with his very astute wife May, five children, two girls and three boys. He had also ensured that they had had a good education, so much so that he had three well trained co-directors in his sons able and ready to carry on his business.

The 'Gold Room' at the Bird owned Hotel. The far wall with the fine panelling was later knocked out to make the bar. This room was in a wrecked state when Tom and May Bird took it back from the Canadian Army. May Bird collected the furniture from house sales and antique dealers and re-furnished the Manor, carrying out all the interior design herself: - courtesy of Mr Anthony Bird OBE©

The present lounge and bar at the Alveston Manor Hotel: - courtesy of the Alveston Manor Hotel & Adrian Wroth – photographer©

The bar and the panelled pillar mark where the 'Gold Room' once existed:- JRH©

Alveston Manor in the 1960s: - courtesy of Mr Anthony Bird OBE©

The Sales details for the Manor from 1928 make for some interesting reading and give an insight into what the Manor House looked like at this time and before the Bird family took over the house and turned it into first a family home and then later a prestigious hotel.

WALKER BARNARD & SON. F. A. I.,

ESTATE OFFICES

STRATFORD – UPON – AVON

Alveston Manor House – Stratford – Upon –Avon

The above is a beautiful old Manor-House – 15th Century – standing in finely timbered and ornamental Ground of about 6 acres – situated adjacent to Town, within easy run of Warwick, Leamington and Birmingham, in the centre of fine hunting district, near Golf Links and good boating. It is approached by carriage drive with Lodge Entrance.

The Accommodation comprises:

On the Ground Floor

Conservatory Entrance – Spacious Entrance

Lounge – 34ft x 19ft with fine open dog grate and French casements, opening on to Lawn, with anteroom adjoining.

Dining Room 17ft x 17ft communicating with the Library 20ft by13ft 6inches. Morning Room 15ft x 13ft communicating with the Billiard Room 28ft x 19ft. Lavatory and W.C. adjoining. The Domestic Offices – conveniently arranged apart from the Living Quarters, include large Kitchen; Servants Hall: Butler's Pantry: Larder: Scullery: Servants W.C. Convenient Outhouses: Wine and Ale Cellars

First Floor – approached by principal & secondary staircases: Drawing Room 29ft x 17ft – fine Tudor panelling.

Seven Bedrooms: 3 Dressing Rooms Two Bathrooms: Two W.C's Second Floor – To Bedrooms: Box and Tank Room.

Several rooms are panelled and fitted with quaint and useful cupboards. The antique staircases are very interesting. It is a Residence that should appeal strongly to lovers of ancient Manor-Houses.

One of the historic staircases in the present Hotel: - courtesy JRH©

Electric Light, Gas, and Company's Water laid on. Modern sanitation.

The Stabling is in character with the house and comprises three Loose Boxes, three stalls, with loft. Harness Room: Garage for four cars: Outbuildings.

The beautiful <u>old-world Gardens</u> are secluded and contain some fine shrubs & stately trees, with Tennis and Croquet Lawns. There is a very productive walled-in Kitchen Garden of about one acre, with <u>Fish Pond.</u> A well-stocked Orchard, Tool House etc.

Price £10.000 – A part of the Park at the rear could also be acquired if necessary

****

The Bird Family has been responsible for many of Stratford-upon-Avon's major developments. *The Maybird Park,* named after the family's mother, May Bird, *Morrisons Shopping Centre* (formerly Safeway) and the recent *Rosebird Centre,* named after Tony and Janet Bird's youngest daughter Rosie. *The Wildmoor Spa,* one of the West Midlands's leading Day Spas, provides health and fitness facilities for 2500 local residents and won the *UK Spa of the Year Award* about six years ago. The Bird Family has also been involved in many other major projects in the town, including hotels and residential developments, regeneration, business parks, office blocks and also agriculture.

Tony Bird was the Chairman of the Trust which rescued and restored *Stoneleigh Abbey* which was a runner up in the *Restoration of the Century Competition* in the *Country Life Magazine.*

Stoneleigh Abbey in Warwickshire: - courtesy of Mr Tony Bird OBE©

A wedding venue at Stoneleigh Abbey showing the magnificently restored interior: - courtesy of Mr Tony Bird©

Tony Bird is also Chairman of the *King Edward VI School Trust* which has recently carried out a restoration of Shakespeare's classroom that has been opened to the public for the first time in 600 years.

The Stoneleigh Abbey restoration was circa £14 million and the restoration of Shakespeare's Schoolroom cost circa £2 million.

The newly restored Shakespeare schoolroom: - courtesy of Mr Tony Bird OBE©

The King Edward VIth School in Stratford-upon-Avon & the Almshouses: - JRH©

An early 1920s view of the Alveston: - courtesy of Michael Careless©

Mrs Kemble in her 'Further Records'- Bentley, 1890, vol. 2 pages 58-59, says of Alveston Manor:

This house is one of the most curious, quaint, picturesque old places I ever saw. It dates back to the thirteenth century. It is low and irregular looking from the outside, with pointed gables and cluster of queer chimney stacks and a good deal of dark wood-carving. One side of the house fronts the River Avon, a stretch of lawn of about an acre lying between the lower windows and the garden gate that opens on to the road and the river, running close by it, parallel to each other. A very fine row of noble old elm trees borders this lawn on either side, and beyond them on one hand is the enclosure wall of the place, and on the other an ancient grass walk, smooth and wide, with a high heavy yew tree hedge evidently of great antiquity, a perfect monk's meditation ground. Beyond this is an orchard bounded by an over-arching avenue of large old filbert trees that form a perfect bower over another wide grass walk. Beyond this is a large kitchen garden with a fine fish pond at the end of it, the monk's fish reservoir in the fishy monkish days.'

Henry James, in his 'Pictures of Places,' Macmillan, 1883, on page 261 says of Alveston Manor:

'If I were to allude to Stratford, it would not be in connection with the fact that Shakespeare came into this world there. It would be rather to speak of a delightful old house near the Avon which struck me as an ideal home of a Shakespeare scholar, or indeed of any passionate lover of the poet. Here with books and memories and the recurring reflection that he had taken his daily walk across the bridge, at which you look

from your window straight down an avenue of fine old trees, with an ever closed gate at the end of them and a carpet of turf stretched over the decent drive – here I say, with old wainscoted chambers to live in, old polished doorsteps to lead you from one to the other, deep window-seats to sit in, with a play on your lap – here a person for whom the cares of life should have resolved themselves into a care for the greatest genius who has represented and ornamented life, might find a very congruous asylum, or speaking a little wider of the mark, the charming rambling, low-gabled many staired, much panelled mansion would be an agreeable home for any person of taste who should prefer an old house to a new. I find I am talking of it quite like an auctioneer, but what I chiefly had at heart was to commemorate the fact that I had lunched there, and while I lunched kept saying to myself that there is nothing in the world so delightful as the happy accidents of English houses.'

There have been many plays, conferences and events which have taken place over the years at the Alveston Manor Hotel. It has always been the centre of entertainment and social life for Stratford. An example of this was an advertisement in 'The Stage' magazine for the 20th March 1969, which advertises *an Easter Writers' Conference with* the following writers being present:

Donald Bull (Doctor Finlay's Casebook), Alan Tarrant (Thames Television), Ursula Bloom (Novelist), Edward Campbell (Fiction Editor for the London Evening News), Perritt Phillips (Editor, Tit-Bits) and Roland Weisz (Features Editor, Women).

The Stage and Television Today – March 1969 – advertising a Writers' Conference at the Alveston – courtesy of Sue Campbell©

Other interesting celebrities have visited the Alveston, including the notorious John Profumo in February 1950.

John Profumo when MP for Stratford speaking at the Alveston Manor. He was elected the MP for the town in February 1950: - courtesy of Mr Anthony Bird OBE©

John Profumo, CBE -30th January 1915 – 9th March 2006

John Profumo was a British politician whose career in government ended after a sexual relationship with the 19 year old Christine Keeler in 1963. Profumo at the time was 48 and Secretary of State for War. It was later alleged that Miss Keeler was also sleeping with the alleged Russian spy Yevgeny Ivanov – which caused a massive public scandal which led not just to the resignation of John Profumo but that of the Conservative Prime Minister Harold Macmillan.

John Profumo: - courtesy of Getty Images©

After his resignation, Profumo worked as a volunteer at Toynbee Hall, a charity in East London and became its chief fundraiser. These charitable activities helped to restore his reputation and he was appointed a Commander of the Order of the British Empire (CBE) by the Queen in 1975.

Toynbee Hall in East London

Toynbee Hall – *is a charitable building situated in Tower Hamlets in the East End of London. It works to bridge the gap between people of all social and financial backgrounds, with a focus on working towards a future without poverty.*

It was the first university-affiliated institution of the worldwide Settlement Movement; a reformist social agenda that strove to get the rich and the poor to live more closely together in an interdependent community. Founded by Canon Samuel Barnett and Henrietta in 1884 on Commercial Street, it was named in memory of their friend and fellow reformer, Oxford historian Arnold Toynbee, who had died the previous year. Built specifically for the charity as a centre for social reform, it remains just as active today.

* *

John Profumo's family home was close to Stratford-upon-Avon at *Avon Carrow*. The estate had been sold to Profumo's father Albert, the Fourth Baron Profumo, in the 1920s. The house is a Grade II listed property built by the war hero and sportsman Cecil Boyle in 1896. Cecil Boyle played international rugby for England, he was also a great cricket player. Today Avon Carrow is split into three homes.

Avon Carrow near Stratford-upon-Avon

* *

The sale of the Alveston Manor Hotel by the Bird Family, who had owned the Manor since 1938, took place on the 29th January, 1962 at the Hotel – a whole era was coming to an end.

Of interest to Antique Collectors and Dealers, Hoteliers and Individuals

By direction of Mr and Mrs W. T. Bird having sold the property

"Alveston Manor,"

STRATFORD-UPON-AVON

AT EXTREMELY SHORT NOTICE

CATALOGUE

Of the

HIGHLY IMPORTANT SALE OF VALUABLE

ANTIQUE, MODERN & REPRODUCTION

FURNITURE

Including fine quality period Furniture with several sets of Chippendale, Sheraton and other fine Dining Chairs, antique oak gate-leg refectory and other Tables, Buhl Cabinets and Tables, William and Mary style Tables and Chairs, Carolean Day-Bed, fine Clocks. Regency pedestal, Dresser, Copper items.

FINE PERSIAN RUGS AND RUNNERS;

COSTLY LARGE WILTON CARPETS,

Axminster and Wilton Carpeting, 30 Lloyd Loom gold wicker chairs etc.

HOTEL FURNISHINGS, PLATE, CHINA AND GLASS

Including furnishings of some 50 bedrooms with almost 100 divan Bedsteads, 320 lots of Linen and Bedding, etc. (Over 750 lots catalogued)

And to offered for sale by auction by

WALKER BARNARD & DOBSON

On the premises

ON MONDAY, 29TH JANUARY, 1962

Commencing at 10.30 a.m. prompt

* *

The Bird Family sold the Alveston Manor Hotel to the *Forte Group* who later became part of the *Trusthouse Forte Group* of companies.

As with William (Tom) Bird, Charles Forte had an amazing life in which the Alveston Manor played a part when he took over the Hotel in the 1960s.

Charles Carmine Forte, Baron Forte of Ripley – 26th

November 1908 – 28th February 2007. – was a Scottish caterer and hotelier of Italian origin who founded the leisure and hotels conglomerate that ultimately became the Forte Group.

Charles Forte was born in Italy at Mortale, now Monforte, Casalattico in the province of Frosinone, Italy in 1908. At the age of four he emigrated to Scotland with his family. Charles was a strict Roman Catholic boy and attended the Alloa Academy and then St. Joseph's College in Dumfries as a boarder; he then went on to spend two years in Rome.

St. Joseph's College in Dumfries, Scotland

After his time in Rome he returned to England and to his family who were now living in Weston super Mare where his father was running a café with two cousins. Charles' first training in the catering and management trade came when he ran the Venetian Lounge in Brighton for a cousin.

Charles Forte, Baron Forte of Ripley

When he was 26, he set up his first 'milk bar' in 1935, the Strand Milk Bar Ltd in Regent Street, after thoroughly researching the location before he started.

Soon after, Charles Forte expanded into the catering and hotel business in which he was extremely able. Unfortunately when World War II started he was interned on the Isle of Man, due to his Italian nationality, but he was released after three months. After the war, his new company became the Forte Holdings Ltd and bought the prestigious Café Royal in 1954. He went on in this decade to open the first catering facility at Heathrow Airport and the first full motorway service station at Newport Pagnell, Buckinghamshire on the MI motorway in 1959. In 1955 he expanded his hospitality empire by purchasing the Hungaria Restaurant in Lower Regent Street, London.

HUNGARIA
The SAFE Restaurant
**Bomb-proof . Splinter-proof . Blast-proof
Gas-proof and BOREDOM PROOF**
We care for your Safety as well as your Pleasure
OWER REGENT STREET, PICCADILLY CIRCUS, W.1

The Hungaria Restaurant in Lower Regent Street, London

In 1970 the Forte Group merged with Trust Houses to become Trusthouse Forte. Through mergers and expansion, Forte expanded the company into a multibillion pound business. His empire included the Alveston Manor Hotel and in his assets he included the 'Little Chef' and 'Happy Eater' roadside restaurants, 'Crest', 'Forte Grand,' Travelodge and Posthouse hotels as well as the wine merchant Grierson-Blumenthal and a major (although non-controlling) stake in the Savoy Hotel in London.

The Savoy Hotel in London

Happy Eater and the five *Welcome Break* service areas were bought from *Hanson Trust PLC* on 1ˢᵗ August 1986. In the 1990s, the company was renamed as *Forte Group plc*.

In 1993, Charles passed control of the company to his son Rocco, but soon the Forte Group were faced with a hostile takeover bid from *'Granada'*. Ultimately Granada succeeded with a £3.9 billion tender offer in January 1996, which left the family with about £350 million in cash.

Sir Rocco Forte and his sister the Hon. Olga Polizzi. Olga is Rocco Forte Hotels' chief designer and is responsible for the design and refurbishment of over 400 hotel rooms a year. One of her most recent projects is the Assila Hotel, Jeddah in Saudi Arabia.

After eight months, Rocco Forte decided to re-enter the hotel industry and founded with his father and one of his sisters, Olga, (interior designer), the 'Rocco Forte Hotels'. Eight months later the group bought their first hotel, the 'Balmoral' in Edinburgh, while the subsequent sale of luxury hotels by Granada saw the company 'Rocco Forte' at the forefront as a buyer.

Today the *Rocco Forte Hotels* are the largest ultra-luxury hotel operators in Europe, with 12 properties in 5 Star and expansion plans around the world.

On the 28ᵗʰ February 2007, Charles Forte died in his sleep at his London home, aged 98. His wife died in 2010 and was buried alongside her husband in West Hampstead Cemetery.

Charles had been knighted by the Queen Mother in 1970 and created a life peer in February 1982 as Baron Forte of Ripley in the County of Surrey. He was also a knight of the 'Sovereign Military Order of Malta.' Rocco himself was knighted in 1995 and his sister Olga became the Hon. Olga Forte CBE. She was married to the late Count Alessandro Polizzi and then the Hon. William Shawcross.

* *

The Alveston Manor Hotel produced a brochure to advertise the Hotel in 1965 when it belonged to the Forte Group- it contains some charming sketches and descriptions.

'Set amongst venerable old trees and ancient lawns (on which the first ever performance of A Midsummer Night's Dream is said to have been enacted), Alveston Manor is a marvellous survival reflecting a fascinating past. Thirteenth century panelling, an Elizabethan Gazebo of great antiquarian interest, Queen Anne stables – these are some of the gems which contribute to the charm of this fine old Manor House': - courtesy of Ann Edwards©

COCKTAIL BAR

'THE ALVESTON MANOR HOTEL, at the foot of the historic Clopton Bridge on the very banks of the Avon, is but a stone's throw from the Royal Shakespeare Theatre.

Originally a 16th century manor house, it is now a hotel of character and charm. The public rooms are furnished in the best traditions of the Elizabethan age but offer all the comforts and luxury that the twentieth century can provide.'

'The restaurant presents the best in modern cuisine against an authentic background of an earlier century.'

'The bedrooms in the Manor House contain genuine period furniture skilfully blended with modern amenities so that the atmosphere of a gracious past is gracefully married to present-day comfort. In the newly-constructed wing of the hotel the bedrooms have been decorated and furnished to the high standards demanded by modern living.'

* *

The price list for the 1965 brochure also makes for some fascinating reading and it is interesting to see that the more expensive suites are priced in guineas:

Manor House	Bed and Breakfast
Single room without bath	65/–
Twin-bedded room without bath	115/–
Single room with bath	85/–
Double-bedded room with bath	
single occupancy	95/–
double occupancy	130/–
Twin-bedded room with bath	
single occupancy	100/–
double occupancy	150/–
New Block	
Single room with bath	75/–
Double-bedded room with bath	115/–
Twin-bedded room with bath	
single occupancy	85/–
double occupancy	125/–
Large room with bath occupied by:	
(a) two persons	130/–
(b) three persons	160/–
(c) four persons	185/–
Queen Anne House and Cedar Block	
Single room without bath	60/–
Twin-bedded room without bath	105/–
Single room with bath	75/–
Twin-bedded room with bath	125/–
Suite : Single	10 gns.
Double	13 gns.
Three...	16 gns.
Four	19 gns.

Meal Rates

Breakfast	8/6	Afternoon Tea	4/6
Luncheon	13/6	Dinner	18/6
	also a la carte		

The above prices are subject to 10% Service Charge

En Pension Terms

Available for stays of three days or longer
Full Pension: add 30/– per person to above terms
Demi Pension: add 15/– per person to above terms

* *

Chapter Six: The Present Hotel

The present hotel is situated only a quarter of a mile from the centre of the historic town of Stratford-upon-Avon in Warwickshire. The hotel commands a grand position looking out over the Clopton Bridge and towards the famous Shakespeare Memorial Theatre.

The Shakespeare Memorial Theatre and Clopton Bridge: - JRH (see colour plate)

As a guest at the Alveston Manor as you walk into the town, you pass the splendid Gower Monument which celebrates William Shakespeare and his importance to the town of Stratford-upon-Avon.

The Gower Monument close to the Alveston Manor Hotel: - JRH

The figures were designed and modelled by Lord Ronald Gower, who presented the monument to the town of Stratford-upon-Avon in 1888. The work was executed in Paris and took 12 years to complete. Associated with Lord Ronald in his task were his assistant Monsieur L. Madrass, the firm of Tassel, who made all the figures save that of Hamlet, which was entrusted to Messieurs Graux and Marley; and the house of De Cauville and Perzinku, who cast the wreathes, the masks, the fruit and the flowers. The stone used in the monument is partly Box ground Bath, partly York. The group was erected in its original site close to the present theatre by Mr Frederick Taylor, contractor, under the supervision of the architects Messieurs Peigniet and Marnay of Paris.

The bronze figures of Falstaff, Hamlet, Prince Henry V & Lady Macbeth surrounding the Gower Monument: - JRH

'The Young Shakespeare' and the bronze statue of 'Hermaphroditus' by J. H. Foley 1844 – both in the park across the river from the Alveston Manor: - JRH©

The statue of William Shakespeare in front of Alveston Manor

The present front entrance to the Alveston Manor Hotel: - JRH

The present building is a wonderful myriad of different historical periods. The Manor Bar contains 16th century panelling; the centre of the house is thought to Elizabethan; the gables nearest the road are from the era of William and Mary and the windows in the centre of the building are Queen Anne.

The Modern Alveston Manor is on the edge of the very busy town of Stratford-upon-Avon and offers all the amenities of a modern 21st Century hotel. The Hotel website gives the potential guests an idea of what they can receive if they book their stay in Stratford at the Alveston Manor:

'The Macdonald Alveston Manor Hotel is one of the finest 4-star hotels in Warwickshire, offering great luxury accommodation in one of the most beautiful and historic parts of England.

Set in the very heart of Shakespeare Country, and in close proximity to beautiful Cotswold villages, the historic Alveston Manor Hotel is set in its own grounds just 5 minutes' walk from all the cultural attractions of Stratford-upon-Avon.

Our hotel in Stratford-upon-Avon is a perfect venue for leisure breaks, romantic weekends, business meetings, weddings and special occasions. We boast excellent hotel accommodation, meeting and event suites, attractive gardens and a luxurious spa.

Macdonald Alveston Manor Hotel is the ideal base for Shakespeare enthusiasts with the Shakespeare Houses and Royal Shakespeare Theatre both nearby. Once you have finished exploring, we recommend a visit to our Vital Health Club for a relaxing sauna before you dine in the fabulous Manor Restaurant.'

Examples of two of the 113 bedrooms at the Alveston Manor Hotel: these are situated in the old stable block - courtesy of Alveston Manor Hotel& Adrian Wroth - photographer©

One of the first class bedrooms in the main hotel: - courtesy of Adrian Wroth-photographer©

The Swimming Pool at the Alveston Manor Spa: - courtesy of the Alveston Manor Hotel& Adrian Wroth - photographer©

The Gym at the Alveston Manor: - courtesy of the Alveston Manor Spa & Adrian Wroth - photographer©

The Cedar Room at the Alveston Manor – ideal venue for weddings, meetings and banqueting: - courtesy of the Alveston Manor Hotel©

The Manor dining room: - courtesy of the Alveston Manor Hotel and Adrian Wroth-photographer©

The Blue Lounge when it was a sitting room in the private house c.1920: - courtesy of Michael Careless©

The 'Blue Lounge' in the present Alveston Manor Hotel: - JRH

The enclosed conservatory which overlooks the back gardens and the 'Kissing Tree': - courtesy of the Alveston Manor Hotel& Adrian Wroth - photographer©

*The modern Alveston Manor Hotel offers facilities for conferences and business meetings: -
courtesy of the Alveston Manor Hotel& Adrian Wroth - photographer©*

After Trusthouse Forte owned and ran the Alveston, the Hotel was run by Forte Granada and then Heritage Hotels before being taken over by Macdonald Hotels in c1992.

The Macdonald Alveston Manor Hotel at Stratford-upon-Avon is run under the company name of *Macdonald Hotels Ltd* which is a hospitality company based in Bathgate, West Lothian in Scotland.

Its main subsidiary, Macdonald Hotels and Resorts, owns or operates hotels and holiday resorts in the United Kingdom and Spain.

* *

Some of the Shakespeare Attractions Close by the Alveston:

The Alveston Manor Hotel is sited within easy walking distance of the Royal Shakespeare Theatre and other museums and associations with William Shakespeare.

The Royal Shakespeare Theatre:

The modern interior of the modern Royal Shakespeare Theatre at Stratford: - courtesy of the Royal Shakespeare Theatre, Stratford, RSC & photograph by Peter Cook©

A performance taking place at the Royal Shakespeare Theatre: - courtesy of the Royal Shakespeare Theatre & photograph by Stewart Hemley© (see colour plate)

The Royal Shakespeare Company officially reopened the newly renovated theatre on the 4th March 2011 when the Queen and Prince Philip attended a performance of the balcony scene from *Romeo and Juliet.*

The £112.8m transformation project included the creation of a new 1040+ seat, thrust auditorium which has brought the actors and the audience much closer together and made the theatre much more like the original Globe Theatre in which Shakespeare's plays were originally performed. In fact the distance of the furthest seat from the stage has been reduced from 27 metres (89ft) to 15 metres (49ft). The Transformation project also included renovation and improvements for the nearby Swan Theatre, a 36 metre (118ft) observation tower, an array of public spaces including a riverside café and Rooftop Restaurant and improved backstage conditions for the actors and crew. The new theatre is also more accessible for people with disabilities.

The Royal Shakespeare Theatre at Stratford-Upon-Avon

Shakespeare's Birthplace: - is a restored 16th century half-timbered building situated in the centre of the town in Henley Street. Here, William Shakespeare spent his childhood years. The house which is open to the public is today owned by the Shakespeare Birthplace Trust.

William Shakespeare's Birthplace in Henley Street, Stratford-upon-Avon

The Birthplace was a substantial house for the time of Shakespeare and would have been originally divided into two, the family living in the one half and Shakespeare's father John Shakespeare could carry on with his glove making and his business as a wool merchant from the same premises.

The house would have been constructed in wattle and daub around a wooden frame. Local oak originated from the Forest of Arden and blue-grey stone would have come locally from Wilmcote. The floor would have been stone flagged and the fireplace constructed of early brick and stone.

Wattle and Daub:

Wattle and daub is a composite building material used for making walls, in which a woven wooden lattice of wooden strips called 'wattle' is daubed with a sticky material made from a combination of wet soil, clay, sand, animal dung and straw.

Shakespeare's Birthplace – Stratford-Upon-Avon

Shakespeare's House in the 19ʰ Century before extensive renovations took place

The Grammar School in Stratford:

We do not know very much about William Shakespeare's education as no records of his attendance have survived but we can make some assumptions that as his father John Shakespeare was elected at one time Alderman in Stratford, this position would also have given his children a free education at the King Edward VI Grammar School from the age of 7 years.

The Grammar School is also referred to as the 'King's New School' as it was named according to a charter by King Edward VI, the son of Henry VIII and Jane Seymour in 1553.

The Grammar School in Stratford where Shakespeare would probably have attended school

Mr Tony Bird OBE whose family owned the *Alveston Manor Hotel* for nearly 30 years is Chairman of the *King Edward VI School Trust* who recently carried out a restoration of Shakespeare's classroom at the old Grammar School. This has been opened to the public for the first time in 600 years.

Shakespeare's classroom at the King Edward VI Grammar School in Stratford: courtesy of Mr Tony Bird OBE©

Mr Anthony Bird OBE also donated the statue of the 'Jester' in Henley Street Stratford, a bronze statue of Shakespeare's 'Henry V' and one of Shakespeare himself sited outside the Town Hall in Stratford. The Bird family have been great benefactors of the town for many years.

The Jester found in Henley Street was commissioned by Anthony Bird OBE 'as a token of his esteem for the town in which he was born lives and works and which has given him so much friendship, good fortune and pleasure.' Anthony Bird is Managing Director of the company Bird Group who also commissioned the statue of Lawrence Olivier as 'Henry V' at the Maybird Shopping Park.

The 'Jester' is constructed of bronze, standing on a stone plinth and features the Jester 'Touchstone' who was in the play 'As you like It' by William Shakespeare. The inscription includes – *'O noble fool, a worthy fool – The fool doth think he is wise but a wise man knows himself to be a fool.'*

The statue was executed by James Butler MBE of Radway and is one of the many fine works by this renowned artist which include carvings and designs of the Queen's Beasts in Kew Gardens, the Royal Seal of the Realm, the Jubilee coin and the 50p coin commemorating Roger Bannister's 4 minute mile.

Mr Anthony Bird OBE also commissioned the full length sculpture, slightly larger than life of Laurence Olivier as 'Henry V'. It shows Henry clad in full armour apart from his helmet which is under his left arm. In his right hand he holds a sword horizontally above his head signalling victory. The statue is outside the Rosebird Shopping Park named after Mr Bird's mother Rose.

The statue of Henry V outside the Rosebird Shopping Park in Stratford

The sculpture is by the Salford born sculptor John Blakeley. John was born in 1928 and trained at Stockport College. He started as a portrait painter then more famously as a bronze cast sculptor.

The 'Henry Vth' sculpture was made over a two year period in his Stockport studio with the assistance of Mike Lloyd-Stafford, a sculptor in his own right.

* *

Acknowledgements:

I would like to thank the Macdonald Group and the Manager and staff at the Alveston Manor Hotel at Stratford-upon-Avon for all their encouragement and support for this book.

Mr Adrian Wroth the photographer who has allowed me to use a selection of his photographs taken for the Alveston Manor Hotel. His generosity is very much appreciated.

My researcher, Sue Campbell for finding some interesting articles, pictures and information for the various chapters in this book.

I am especially grateful to Mrs Jane Cox who has again carried out the often difficult and challenging task of proofreading and for her advice and positive comments which have made this book a great pleasure to research and to write.

A grateful thanks to Mr Roger Morris for his excellent oil painting of the Alveston Manor Hotel which has been used for the cover of this book. The cover design was taken from a photograph by Adrian Wroth with his kind permission.

Kathryn Baker, her mother Joan and father Ed at 'Paper and Card' for helping to format the cover and to check for corrections before submitting this to the printer. For helping to ensure the photographs and diagrams in the book have been improved and enhanced where this was required. Their support and encouragement are very much appreciated.

To Mr Tony Bird OBE for his valuable and most interesting memories of living at the Manor as a boy with his family and all the associations and history of the Manor which have proved so interesting in Chapter 5 in particular. Both Mr Bird and his secretary Claire have put up with my questions, e-mails and visits with great patience and made Chapter Five one of the most interesting chapters in this book.

The Shakespeare Birthplace Trust Archives for their support and allowing me to use their material associated with the Alveston Manor.

Chapter One: Early History of the Alveston

Extract from the Osteological Analysis Alveston Manor Hotel: SAM02 NGR: SP 2087 5473 Report No 0607 May 2007.

Thanks to Dr David Morrison at the Worcester Cathedral Library for the following references:

The Victoria County History of Warwickshire-Volume 2 p97. James Street, London 1906 & Sir William Dugdale's Antiquities of Warwickshire Volume 2- published by John Osborn and Thomas Longman in London in 1730. Various other documents and Rolls and references to Francesca Tinti in her book 'Sustaining Belief' – The Church of Worcester from c870 to c1100 published by Ashgate at Farnham in 2010, pp201-203.

The Cathedral Library and volunteer Vanda Bartoszuk for finding the following references to Alveston and the Manor: 1. Liber Albus WCM A5 (1301-1450) folio 104a Dated 1321. 2. Worcester Monastic Registers WCM A6 (i) (1458-1498) folio 73 & 3. WCM A6 (i) folio 6V – dated 1459.

Chapter Two: Later History of the Manor

British History online – The Victoria County History.

http://www.historyofparliamentonline.org/volume/1558-1603/member/greville-edward-1622

A History of the County of Warwick: Volume 3, Barlichway Hundred. Originally published by Victoria County History, London, 1945.

Lordship, Knighthood and Locality: A study in English Society, C1180-1280.

The painting, Will and history of Colonel Newsham Peers – by kind permission of the trustees of the Royal Welch Fusiliers Regimental Museum, Caernarfon.

Mr Brian Johnson of the Old Church Alveston for the photograph of Col. Newsham Peers.

Description of Colonel Newsham Peers's will from the National Archives at Kew.

Historic England.

Mr Andrew Bridges for his postcards which he has kindly allowed me to use in this chapter.

Mr Brian Johnson of Alveston for his suggestions, pictures and information for this chapter. His support is very much appreciated.

Chapter Three: The Manor House

The Manager and staff at the Alveston Manor Hotel for their hospitality and support in the researching of this book.

Historic England: List No: 1281377 on Alveston Manor.

Mr A.P.S de Redman, FSA Scot., Hon., FHS., Birmingham City Honorary Armorist for the research he carried out on my behalf to interpret the Heraldic Shields at Alveston Manor.

Chapter Four: The Gardens

The Shakespeare Birthplace Trust Archives for their research and extracts which I have used in this chapter. Their time and support on my behalf are very much appreciated.

The photographs by Adrian Wroth taken for the Alveston Manor Hotel, which I have been kindly allowed to reproduce.

Chapter Five: The Past Hotel

I am extremely grateful to Mr Anthony Bird OBE for his support and encouragement in the writing of this chapter. He has given generously of his time and allowed me to include photographs and documents which have made this chapter so interesting. I would also like to thank most sincerely Mr Bird's secretary Claire who has put up with my enquiries, many e-mails and phone calls to arrange meetings and scan documents from Mr Bird.

Acknowledging David Warner for 'WW2 People's War' extract for this chapter.

Chapter Six: The Present Alveston Manor Hotel

The Regional General Manager and all his staff at the Alveston Manor Hotel for their much valued support and encouragement for this book. On my various visits to the hotel I have always been made very welcome and my questions and enquiries have been answered in a really efficient manner and for this I am extremely grateful.

To Mr Brian Thomas in charge of maintenance and one of the longest serving members of staff and Mr Michael Careless the Night Manager for their support for the book and for information and photographs which have made this book so much more interesting.

The Macdonald Group for giving me some information on the company who presently own the Alveston Manor Hotel, which I have found extremely useful and for their support and encouragement for the book.

Mr Adrian Wroth the photographer, who has allowed me to use his photographs of the hotel without restriction, his kindness is very much appreciated.

* *